THE EYE *of* GOD

Toney James

AF415071

PUBLISHED BY   STANDING TREE PUBLISHING

AUTHOR: Toney James
TYPESETTING: Brandon Daniel

COVER PHOTO: Hubble Helix Nebula (NGC 7293)
The Helix Nebula is an example of a planetary nebula. Though it looks like a bubble or eye from Earth's point of view, the Helix is actually a trillion-mile-long tunnel of glowing gases. In its center lies a white dwarf star.

IMAGE CREDIT: NASA, NOAO, ESA, the Hubble Helix Nebula Team, M. Meixner (STScI), and T.A. Rector (NRAO).

ISBN HARDBACK: 979-8-9961460-1-7
ISBN PAPERBACK: 979-8-2340730-8-2
ISBN EBOOK: 979-8-9961460-0-0
ISBN AUDIOBOOK: 979-8-9961460-2-4

THE EYE *of* GOD

A Journey Through Consciousness, Reality, and Divine Purpose

TONEY JAMES

DEDICATION

To every consciousness that has ever wondered why it exists, To every witness who has turned on the lights in the darkness, To every seeker who has knocked on the doors of understanding, And to the Architect, who loved us enough to create a universe just so we could find our way home.

CONTENTS

PREFACE: A LETTER TO THE SEEKER

Dear Reader,

You hold in your hands a book that has been both written and discovered. I say "discovered" because the ideas contained here do not originate with me—they have always existed, waiting in the darkness like that blue ball we will soon discuss, needing only a witness to bring them into the light.

This is not a book of answers. It is a book of better questions.

If you have picked up this volume, you are likely someone who has felt the peculiar ache of consciousness—the strange burden and gift of being aware that you are aware. You have probably lain awake at night wondering why there is something rather than nothing, why you exist at this particular moment in cosmic history, and whether your choices matter in a universe that seems to operate according to laws you did not write.

You are a seeker. And this book is written for you.

I must warn you: what follows will challenge some of your most fundamental assumptions about reality. We will explore ideas that may initially seem contradictory—that you are both free and predetermined, both separate and connected, both temporary and eternal. We will examine the possibility that the universe is not a random accident but an intentional classroom, designed by an Architect who knows you more intimately than you know yourself.

Some of these ideas will resonate immediately, striking a chord of recognition deep within you. Others will resist, creating friction against your current understanding. Both responses are valuable. Truth often announces itself through resonance, but it also reveals itself through resistance—the places where our comfortable beliefs are challenged are often the places where growth awaits.

This book is structured as a journey, moving from foundational questions about consciousness and reality toward increasingly practical questions about how to live as a spiritual being in a material world. You may read it sequentially, allowing each chapter to build upon the last, or you may find yourself drawn to particular chapters that address your current questions. Trust your intuition. The Architect speaks through many voices, including the quiet voice of your own curiosity.

Throughout these pages, I use the term "the Architect" to refer to the divine intelligence that has designed this universe. You may know this presence by other names—God, the Divine, the Source, the Ground of Being. The name matters less than the recognition: there is an intelligence behind existence, and that intelligence is not indifferent to you.

I also use "we" language extensively. This is intentional. I am not writing as an expert who has arrived at some final destination, dispensing wisdom from on high. I am a fellow traveler, someone who has wrestled with these questions and continues to wrestle with them. The insights offered here have been hard-won through years of contemplation, study, suffering, and grace. But they remain insights, not certainties—glimpses of truth seen through the veil of human limitation.

You will notice that this book draws from multiple wells: quantum physics and cosmology, ancient philosophy and modern theology, mystical experience and rational analysis. This is because truth is not the exclusive property of any single discipline. The Architect has left fingerprints everywhere, and we must be willing to look in unexpected places.

Some readers will approach this book primarily through the intellect, seeking logical coherence and philosophical rigor. Others will approach it through the heart, seeking spiritual nourishment and existential comfort. Both approaches are valid. In fact, the deepest truths require both mind and heart, both analysis and intuition. Try to engage with these ideas on multiple levels simultaneously.

At the end of each major section, you will find space for reflection—not formal questions to answer, but invitations to pause and allow the ideas to settle. I encourage you to take these pauses seriously. Spiritual understanding is not merely intellectual assent; it is a transformation of consciousness that requires time and stillness.

Finally, I want to address the question you may already be asking: "Is this book true?"

The answer is both simpler and more complex than you might expect. The metaphors and frameworks presented here are models—ways of pointing toward realities that exceed our capacity for direct description. The map is not the territory. The menu is not the meal. But a good map can guide you toward the territory, and a good menu can help you order the meal.

What I can promise you is this: if you engage with these ideas sincerely, if you allow them to challenge and expand your understanding, you will not finish this book as the same person who began it. The movie does not change, but the movie changes you.

The Architect is waiting. The classroom is in session. The lights are ready to be turned on.
Let us begin.

With hope and humility, Toney James

INTRODUCTION: HOW TO READ THIS BOOK

This book is designed to be experienced, not merely consumed.

In our age of information abundance, we have become skilled at extracting data, skimming for key points, and moving quickly from one idea to the next. This approach serves us well in many contexts, but it will not serve you here. The ideas in this book are not data points to be collected; they are invitations to transformation.

READ SLOWLY

The chapters that follow contain dense philosophical and theological concepts, but they are not meant to be difficult for difficulty's sake. They are meant to be deep. Depth requires time. A single paragraph may contain an idea worth contemplating for days or weeks.

I encourage you to read with a pen in hand. Underline passages that resonate. Write questions in the margins. Argue with the text. The most valuable reading is active reading, where you are in dialogue with the ideas rather than passively receiving them.

EXPECT DISCOMFORT

If you find yourself feeling uncomfortable, confused, or even resistant at certain points, do not assume you are reading incorrectly. Discomfort is often a sign that you are approaching the edges of your current understanding—and edges are where growth happens. Some of the ideas presented here may conflict with beliefs you have held for years. You may feel the urge to dismiss them quickly or to defend your existing framework. I ask you to resist that urge, at least temporarily. Hold the new idea alongside your existing belief without immediately resolving the tension. Paradox is not always a problem to be solved; sometimes it is a doorway to be entered.

ENGAGE MULTIPLE WAYS OF KNOWING

This book addresses both the rational mind and the intuitive heart. Some chapters will appeal more to logical analysis; others will speak more to direct spiritual experience. Try to remain open to both modes of understanding.

When you encounter a metaphor—the sealed room, the finished film, the cosmic classroom—do not merely analyze it intellectually. Allow yourself to enter the metaphor imaginatively. What does it feel like to be a witness in the void? What sensations arise when you consider yourself as a character in a predetermined story? Embodied understanding often precedes intellectual comprehension.

USE THE REFLECTION SPACES

Throughout the book, you will find natural pauses—places where the text invites you to stop and reflect. These are not interruptions; they are essential parts of the journey. Spiritual transformation requires integration time, moments when new ideas can settle into your consciousness and begin their work of reorganization.

Consider keeping a journal alongside your reading. After each chapter, spend time writing about what resonated, what confused you, what questions arose, and what you noticed about your own reactions. The book you write in response to this book may ultimately be more valuable than the book itself.

RETURN AND REVISIT

This is not a book you will fully understand on first reading. Nor is it meant to be. Spiritual texts reveal themselves in layers, offering different insights depending on where you are in your own journey.

You may find that a passage that seemed opaque on first encounter becomes luminous six months later, after you have lived with the ideas and allowed them to work on you. Or a chapter that initially seemed simple may reveal unexpected depths upon return.

Think of this book as a companion for your spiritual journey rather than a destination. It is meant to be returned to, reread, and reconsidered as you grow and change.

TRUST THE STRUCTURE

The book is organized intentionally, moving from foundational metaphysical questions toward increasingly practical spiritual concerns. Part I establishes the nature of consciousness and reality. Part II explores the purpose and design of existence. Part III offers practices for living as an awakened being. Part IV maps the journey of spiritual maturation.

While you may be tempted to skip ahead to the "practical" chapters, I encourage you to trust the progression. The practices in Part III will make more sense—and be more transformative—if you have first grappled with the philosophical foundations in Parts I and II. The map in Part IV will be more useful if you have first understood the territory it describes.

That said, if you find yourself genuinely stuck in a particular chapter, it is acceptable to move forward and return later. Sometimes understanding comes in non-linear ways, and a later chapter may illuminate an earlier one.

READ IN COMMUNITY (IF POSSIBLE)

While this book can certainly be read in solitude, there is particular value in reading it alongside others. The discussion questions in the back matter are designed for spiritual study groups, book clubs, or informal gatherings of seekers. When we articulate our understanding to others, we often discover what we truly think. When we hear others' interpretations, we encounter perspectives we would never have reached alone. The Architect speaks through community as well as through solitude.

If you do not have a ready-made community for this kind of

exploration, consider forming one. Invite a few friends or acquaintances who share your spiritual hunger. Meet regularly to discuss a chapter at a time. You may be surprised by how hungry others are for this kind of deep conversation.

BRING YOUR WHOLE SELF

Finally, and most importantly: bring your whole self to this reading. Bring your doubts and your faith, your intellect and your intuition, your wounds and your wisdom. Bring your questions, especially the ones you have been afraid to ask aloud.

This book does not require you to abandon your critical thinking or to accept ideas on blind faith. It invites you to think more deeply, to question more honestly, and to remain open to possibilities you may have previously dismissed.

The Architect does not fear your questions. The truth does not require your protection. You are invited to bring your full, authentic self to this exploration—including the parts of yourself that are skeptical, confused, or resistant.

A NOTE ON LANGUAGE

Throughout this book, I use gendered pronouns for the Architect (He/Him), following traditional theological language. This is a limitation of human language rather than a claim about the nature of the Divine. The Architect transcends gender, transcends all categories we might use to contain or describe ultimate reality.

If this language creates barriers for you, I invite you to mentally substitute whatever terms feel most authentic to your understanding. What matters is not the pronoun but the recognition of a personal, loving intelligence behind existence.

BEGIN WHEN YOU ARE READY

There is no perfect time to begin a spiritual journey. There is no moment when you will feel completely prepared, completely open, completely ready for transformation.

But there is this moment. And this moment is enough.

The void is waiting. The witness is needed. The Architect has prepared a classroom, and you have been invited to attend.

Turn the page when you are ready.The lights are about to come on.

PART I

THE FOUNDATIONS OF REALITY

CHAPTER 1

THE VOID AND THE WITNESS

> "In the beginning was the Word,
> and the Word was with God,
> and the Word was God."
> — John 1:1

We begin in darkness.

Not the darkness of a moonless night, where your eyes might eventually adjust and discern shapes and shadows. Not the darkness of a closed room, where a sliver of light beneath the door promises illumination beyond. We begin in absolute darkness—a sealed void where light has never entered and cannot enter, where the very concept of sight has no meaning.

In this darkness, there is a ball.

The ball is blue. Or rather, the ball has the physical properties that, when light strikes it, would reflect wavelengths we perceive as blue. But in this sealed darkness, no light strikes it. No eye observes it. No consciousness names it.

Is the ball blue?

This is not a trick question, though it may feel like one. It is an invitation to examine the relationship between physical reality and conscious observation—a relationship that lies at the very foundation of existence itself.

Your first instinct might be to say: "Of course the ball is blue. Its molecular structure determines which wavelengths it reflects. The blueness is an objective property of the object, independent of whether anyone observes it."

This is a reasonable answer. It is the answer most of us have been taught. It is also, I will suggest, incomplete.

Consider: what does it mean for something to be blue if no consciousness ever experiences that blueness? The wavelengths exist, yes. The molecular structure exists. But "blue"—the quale, the subjective experience of blueness—exists only in the presence of a witness.

Without consciousness, there is no color. There is only electromagnetic radiation of varying frequencies, interacting with matter in predictable ways. The universe does not "see" blue. It does not experience anything. It simply is—a vast field of potential, waiting.

Waiting for what?

Waiting for a witness.

1.1 THE THOUGHT EXPERIMENT OF DARKNESS

Let us stay with this image a while longer, because it contains more than it first appears to contain. Imagine you are given the power to enter this sealed void. You bring with you a flashlight. Before you turn it on, you stand in the absolute darkness, knowing that somewhere in this space, there is a blue ball.

In this moment before illumination, what exists?

The ball exists, certainly, as a physical object with mass and molecular structure. The space exists. You exist. But the relationship between you and the ball—the relationship that would allow you to say "I see a blue ball"—does not yet exist.

Now you turn on the flashlight.

Light floods the space. Photons strike the ball, are absorbed and reflected according to its molecular properties. The reflected light enters your eyes, strikes your retinas, triggers electrochemical signals that travel to your visual cortex. And in that moment, something extraordinary happens.

The ball becomes blue.

Not just to you, but in a more fundamental sense: the potential for blueness that existed in the darkness is actualized through the act of observation. The physical properties of the ball have not changed—but the reality of the ball has changed. It has moved from potential to actual, from abstract to concrete, from unknown to known. You have not created the ball. But you have, in a very real sense, created its blueness. Or more precisely: you have participated with the ball in bringing blueness into existence.

This is the first great mystery: consciousness does not merely observe reality; it participates in actualizing reality.

THE QUANTUM ECHO

If this sounds strange, even mystical, consider that modern physics has arrived at a similar conclusion through a very different route.

In quantum mechanics, particles exist in a state of superposition—multiple potential states simultaneously—until they are observed. The famous double-slit experiment demonstrates this beautifully: a photon behaves as both a particle and a wave until the moment of measurement, at which point it "collapses" into one definite state.

The act of observation does not merely reveal which state the photon was in; it participates in determining which state the photon is in.

This is not mysticism. This is experimental fact, replicated thousands of times in laboratories around the world. The observer effect is not a bug in our measurement tools; it is a fundamental feature of reality itself.

Now, quantum physicists debate what this means. Some argue for the Copenhagen interpretation, which suggests that consciousness collapses the wave function. Others prefer the many-worlds interpretation, which suggests that all possible states occur in branching universes. Still others propose various forms of objective collapse theories.

But beneath these debates lies a common recognition: the relationship between observer and observed is not incidental to reality. It is constitutive of reality.

The ball in the darkness is not simply waiting to be discovered. It is waiting to be actualized through the presence of a witness.

THE PHILOSOPHICAL TRADITION

This insight is not new, though quantum mechanics has given it new language and new urgency.

The philosopher George Berkeley argued in the 18th century that "to be is to be perceived"—that objects have no existence independent of minds that perceive them. His idealism was radical, suggesting that the entire material world exists only as ideas in the mind of God and in the minds of conscious observers. Most of us instinctively resist this conclusion. It feels solipsistic, as though we are claiming to create reality through our thoughts. But Berkeley was not suggesting that individual human minds create the world. He was suggesting that consciousness—including and especially divine consciousness—is the ground of all being.

Immanuel Kant approached the question differently but arrived at a related insight. He distinguished between the "thing-in-itself" (the noumenon) and the "thing-as-it-appears-to-us" (the phenomenon). We can never know the thing-in-itself directly; we can only know it as it appears through the structures of our consciousness—through space, time, causality, and the other categories through which we organize experience.

The ball in the darkness is the thing-in-itself. The blue ball illuminated by your flashlight is the phenomenon. And the gap between them is bridged by consciousness.

More recently, phenomenologists like Edmund Husserl and Martin Heidegger have explored the structure of consciousness and its relationship to being. Husserl spoke of "intentionality"—the fact that consciousness is always consciousness of something, always directed toward an object. Heidegger spoke of "being-in-the-world"—the fact that we are not detached observers of reality but participants embedded within it. These philosophical traditions, diverse as they are, share a common recognition: the relationship between consciousness and reality is not external and accidental. It is internal and essential.

THE THEOLOGICAL DIMENSION

Now we arrive at the deepest layer of our thought experiment.

If consciousness is required to actualize reality—to turn potential into actual, to make the ball blue—then we must ask: what consciousness actualized reality before human consciousness existed?

The universe is approximately 13.8 billion years old. Conscious observers—at least of the human variety—have existed for only a tiny fraction of that time. For billions of years, stars formed and died, galaxies spun, planets coalesced, all without human witnesses.

Was the universe real during those billions of years? Were stars actually bright, or did they merely have the potential for brightness, waiting for eyes that would not evolve for eons?

This is where the thought experiment opens onto theological territory.

The traditional answer, found in various forms across religious traditions, is that divine consciousness has always been present. God is the eternal witness, the primordial observer whose consciousness grounds all of reality.

In the beginning was the Word—the divine utterance that speaks reality into being. And the Word was with God, and the Word was God. Consciousness and being are not separate; they are two aspects of the same ultimate reality.

The ball in the darkness is blue because God sees it as blue. The stars are bright because divine consciousness witnesses their brightness. The universe is real because it exists in the mind of the Architect.

And when human consciousness emerged—when the first creature became aware that it was aware—something new happened. The Architect invited a created consciousness to participate in the work of witnessing. We were given the extraordinary privilege and responsibility of turning on the lights, of naming the colors, of actualizing the potential that had been prepared for us.

This is what Genesis means when it says that Adam named the animals. Naming is not merely labeling; it is a creative act, a participation in bringing order and meaning to the chaos of pure potential. We are not the source of reality. But we are invited to be witnesses to reality, and in witnessing, we participate in making it real.

THE INVITATION

Return to the image of yourself standing in the darkness, flashlight in hand.

Before you turn on the light, you might feel a moment of hesitation. Once you illuminate the space, once you see the blue ball, you cannot unsee it. You will have entered into a relationship with it. You will have taken responsibility for knowing it.

This is the existential situation of consciousness itself.

We did not ask to be born. We did not choose to be witnesses. But here we are, flashlights in hand, standing in the darkness of a vast and mysterious universe.

We can choose to turn on the light or to leave it off. We can choose to witness or to remain in ignorance. We can choose to participate in actualizing reality or to sleepwalk through existence, never fully present to the extraordinary gift and burden of consciousness.

The Architect has created a universe full of potential—stars and planets, mountains and oceans, other conscious beings, beauty and terror and mystery beyond measure. But potential is not enough. Potential requires actualization.

And so the Architect invites us: turn on the light. Name the colors. Witness the world. Participate in the ongoing creation of reality.

This is not optional, not really. To be conscious is to be a witness. The question is only whether we will be conscious witnesses—aware of our role, intentional in our participation—or unconscious ones, stumbling through the darkness, never realizing the power and responsibility we carry.

The ball is waiting in the darkness.

The flashlight is in your hand.

What will you do?

1.2 CONSCIOUSNESS AS THE ACTUALIZER OF REALITY

We have established that consciousness plays a role in actualizing reality—in transforming potential into actual, in making the ball blue. But we must go deeper. We must examine what consciousness is and how it performs this extraordinary function.

This is treacherous territory. Consciousness is the one thing we know most intimately and understand least completely. You are conscious right now, reading these words, aware of your awareness. But if I ask you to explain what consciousness is, you will likely find yourself grasping for words, using metaphors and analogies that never quite capture the thing itself.

This is not a failure of intelligence. It is a structural limitation. Consciousness is the lens through which we know everything else; it is extraordinarily difficult to turn that lens back on itself.

Nevertheless, we must try.

THE HARD PROBLEM

The philosopher David Chalmers famously distinguished between the "easy problems" of consciousness and the "hard problem."

The easy problems (which are not actually easy, just more tractable) involve explaining the various functions of consciousness: how the brain processes information, how it integrates sensory data, how it produces behavior, how it enables learning and memory. These are problems of mechanism, and while they are enormously complex, they are in principle solvable through neuroscience and cognitive science.

The hard problem is different. The hard problem is: why is there subjective experience at all? Why does information processing feel like something? Why is there an inner life, a first-person perspective, a "what it is like" to be conscious? You could, in principle, imagine a universe where information processing happens without any accompanying experience—where brains do everything they do, but the lights are off inside, where there is no one home. Such beings would be philosophical zombies: functionally identical to conscious beings but lacking any inner life.

Why aren't we zombies? Why is there something it is like to be you?

This is the hard problem, and it remains unsolved. Neuroscience can map the neural correlates of consciousness—the brain states that accompany conscious experience—but correlation is not explanation. Knowing that certain patterns of neural firing accompany the experience of seeing blue does not explain why those patterns feel like anything at all.

Some philosophers and scientists argue that consciousness is an emergent property of complex information processing—that when a system reaches a certain threshold of complexity and integration, subjective experience simply arises. Others argue that consciousness is fundamental, not emergent—that it is a basic feature of reality, like mass or charge, and that complex brains do not create consciousness but rather tune into it or channel it. I lean toward the latter view, for reasons that will become clear. But for now, simply notice this: consciousness is not reducible to its physical substrate. There is something about subjective experience that exceeds and transcends the material processes that enable it.

THE STRUCTURE OF EXPERIENCE

Even if we cannot fully explain consciousness, we can examine its structure—the way it organizes and presents reality to us.

Phenomenologists have done extensive work on this. They have identified several key features of conscious experience:

Intentionality: Consciousness is always directed toward something. You are never simply conscious; you are always conscious of something—a thought, a sensation, a memory, an object in the world.

Even in states of meditation where the mind seems empty, there is still the awareness of emptiness, the consciousness of consciousness itself.

Temporality: Consciousness exists in time, but not in the simple way that physical objects exist in time. When you experience the present moment, you are not experiencing a knife-edge instant with no duration. You are experiencing a "specious present" that includes retention of the immediate past and protention toward the immediate future. You hear a melody, not just a single note; you read a sentence, not just a single word. Consciousness synthesizes time, creating continuity from discrete moments.

Embodiment: Consciousness is not a disembodied ghost in a machine. It is always situated in a body, experiencing the world from a particular location and perspective. Your consciousness is shaped by your sensory organs, your nervous system, your physical needs and limitations. You do not observe the world from nowhere; you observe it from here, from this body, at this moment.

Intersubjectivity: Consciousness is not solitary. From the beginning, we are aware of other consciousnesses, other perspectives, other witnesses. We learn to see ourselves as others see us. We internalize social norms and expectations. Our consciousness is shaped by language, culture, and relationship. We are not isolated minds; we are nodes in a network of consciousness.

These features are not incidental. They are the structure through which reality appears to us. And because consciousness actualizes reality—because the ball becomes blue through the act of witnessing— these features of consciousness shape the reality that is actualized.

THE CREATIVE ACT OF PERCEPTION

Here is where we must challenge a common assumption: that perception is passive, that consciousness is like a mirror reflecting reality as it is.

This is not how perception works.

When you look at a tree, you do not simply receive data about the tree. Your brain actively constructs the experience of the tree, using sensory input as raw material but adding interpretation, context, meaning. Your visual system fills in blind spots, corrects for distortions, makes assumptions about depth and distance. Your conceptual system categorizes the tree, distinguishes it from its background, relates it to other trees you have seen.

The tree you experience is not the tree-in-itself. It is the tree-as-constructed-by-your-consciousness.

This is not to say the tree is unreal or that you are hallucinating. The tree exists independently of your perception. But the tree-as-you-experience-it is a collaboration between the physical tree and your consciousness. It is a creative act, not a passive reception.

Now extend this insight. If every act of perception is creative, if consciousness actively constructs the reality it experiences, then consciousness is not merely observing a pre-existing reality. It is participating in the ongoing creation of reality. The ball in the darkness has certain physical properties. But "blue" is not simply a property of the ball. "Blue" is what happens when those physical properties encounter a consciousness capable of experiencing blueness. Blue is a collaboration between matter and mind.

And if this is true of blue, it is true of everything else. The warmth of sunlight, the taste of bread, the sound of music, the feeling of love—all of these are collaborations between physical reality and conscious experience. They are actualized through the meeting of matter and mind.

THE WITNESS AS CO-CREATOR

This brings us to a startling conclusion: to be a witness is to be a co-creator.

Not in the sense that we create reality ex nihilo, out of nothing. The Architect has done that. The physical universe exists independently of human consciousness, governed by laws we did not write.

But in the sense that we participate in determining what kind of reality the physical universe becomes. We actualize certain potentials and leave others dormant. We bring certain aspects of reality into the light and leave others in darkness. Consider two people walking through the same forest. One is a botanist, trained to notice and name plant species. The other is a poet, attuned to beauty and metaphor. They walk the same path, but they actualize different realities. The botanist sees taxonomy, ecological relationships, evolutionary adaptations. The poet sees symbols, emotions, spiritual truths.

Which one sees the "real" forest?

Both do. And neither does. The forest-in-itself exceeds both perspectives. But the forest-as-experienced is different for each witness, because each witness brings different capacities, different frameworks, different intentions to the act of observation.

This is not relativism. It is not the claim that all perspectives are equally valid or that truth is merely subjective. Some perspectives are more accurate, more comprehensive, more aligned with reality than others.

But it is the recognition that reality is not a fixed, static thing that exists independently of all observation. Reality is dynamic, relational, participatory. It is what happens when consciousness encounters the physical world and actualizes certain potentials.

And this means that the quality of our consciousness matters. The depth of our attention, the breadth of our awareness, the clarity of our perception—these shape the reality we actualize.

A distracted consciousness actualizes a thin, superficial reality. A deep, attentive consciousness actualizes a rich, multidimensional reality.

A fearful consciousness actualizes a threatening reality. A loving consciousness actualizes a beautiful reality.

We are not passive observers. We are active participants in the ongoing creation of the world.

THE RESPONSIBILITY OF WITNESSING

This is an awesome responsibility.

If consciousness actualizes reality, then we bear responsibility for the reality we bring into being. We cannot blame the world for being ugly if we have witnessed it with ugly consciousness. We cannot complain that life is meaningless if we have failed to bring meaning to our witnessing.

This does not mean we are responsible for everything that happens. We did not create the laws of physics. We did not design the structure of the universe. We are not the Architect.

But we are responsible for how we participate in the reality the Architect has created. We are responsible for what we notice and what we ignore, what we name and what we leave unnamed, what we bring into the light and what we leave in darkness.

The ball in the darkness is waiting. It has the potential to be blue, but that potential will not actualize itself. It requires a witness.

And not just any witness. It requires a witness who is present, attentive, willing to see. A witness who brings the light and does not flinch from what the light reveals.

This is the calling of consciousness: to witness reality fully, honestly, courageously. To actualize the potential that the Architect has embedded in creation. To participate in the ongoing work of bringing order from chaos, meaning from randomness, beauty from raw material.

We did not ask for this calling. But we have received it nonetheless.

The question is: will we answer?

1.3 THE INVITATION TO WITNESS

We have explored the metaphysics of witnessing—the way consciousness actualizes reality, the creative nature of perception, the participatory relationship between observer and observed. Now we must make this personal. You are a witness. Not in theory, but in fact. Right now, in this moment, you are actualizing reality through your consciousness.

The words on this page are black marks on white paper (or pixels on a screen). But they become meaningful through your witnessing. You bring to them your language, your concepts, your history, your questions. And in that meeting between text and consciousness, meaning emerges—meaning that did not exist in the marks alone, nor in your mind alone, but in the relationship between them.

This is happening constantly, in every moment of your waking life. You are continuously actualizing reality through your attention, your perception, your consciousness.

But most of the time, you do this unconsciously. You witness on autopilot, using habitual patterns of perception, seeing what you expect to see, filtering reality through unexamined assumptions.

The invitation is to become a conscious witness—to bring awareness to the act of witnessing itself, to take responsibility for the reality you are actualizing.

THE PRACTICE OF ATTENTION

Conscious witnessing begins with attention. Attention is the focusing of consciousness, the directing of awareness toward a particular object or aspect of experience. It is the flashlight beam in the darkness, illuminating one area while leaving others in shadow.

We tend to think of attention as a limited resource, something we must conserve and allocate carefully. And in one sense, this is true. You cannot pay full attention to everything simultaneously. Attention requires selection, prioritization, focus.

But in another sense, attention is not a resource that depletes with use. It is a capacity that strengthens with practice. The more you practice paying attention, the more capable of attention you become.

Consider the difference between a novice and an expert in any field. The novice looks at a chess board and sees pieces. The expert sees patterns, strategies, possibilities. The novice listens to a symphony and hears sounds. The expert hears themes, variations, harmonic relationships.

The difference is not in the raw sensory data. The difference is in the quality of attention brought to that data.

The expert has trained their attention, refined it, deepened it. They have learned to notice what the novice misses. They actualize a richer, more complex reality from the same physical stimuli.

This is true not just in specialized domains but in life itself. You can move through your days with shallow, scattered attention, barely present to your experience. Or you can cultivate deep, sustained attention, fully present to each moment.

The reality you actualize will be radically different depending on which path you choose.

SEEING WHAT IS THERE

Conscious witnessing requires seeing what is actually there, not what you expect or want to see.

This is harder than it sounds. Our perception is shaped by countless filters: our beliefs, our fears, our desires, our cultural conditioning, our past experiences. We see through these filters, often without realizing they are there.

A simple example: if you believe the world is fundamentally hostile, you will notice threats and dangers everywhere. Your attention will be drawn to anything that confirms your belief, and you will overlook or minimize evidence to the contrary. You will actualize a hostile reality, not because the world is objectively hostile, but because your consciousness is tuned to hostility. Conversely, if you believe the world is fundamentally benevolent, you will notice kindness and beauty. You will actualize a benevolent reality.

Both witnesses are looking at the same physical world. But they are actualizing different realities because they are bringing different consciousness to their witnessing.

The practice of seeing what is there requires becoming aware of your filters and learning to set them aside, at least temporarily. It requires a kind of radical openness, a willingness to be surprised, to have your expectations overturned, to encounter reality on its own terms rather than on yours.

This is what the Zen tradition calls "beginner's mind"—approaching each moment as if for the first time, without preconceptions or assumptions. It is what the Christian mystics call "purity of heart"—a single-minded focus on truth, undistorted by selfish desire or fear.

It is extraordinarily difficult. Our filters are deeply ingrained, often unconscious. We have spent our entire lives learning to see the world in certain ways, and those ways have become automatic, invisible.

But it is possible. Through practice, through discipline, through grace, we can learn to see more clearly. We can learn to witness what is actually there.

NAMING WITH CARE

Conscious witnessing also requires careful naming.

Remember: naming is not merely labeling. It is a creative act, a way of bringing order and meaning to experience. When Adam named the animals, he was not simply assigning arbitrary sounds to creatures. He was discerning their essence, their nature, their place in the created order.

We name constantly, usually without thinking about it. We name our experiences: "This is good." "This is bad." "This is boring." "This is exciting." We name other people: "She is kind." "He is selfish." "They are trustworthy." We name ourselves: "I am successful." "I am a failure." "I am loved." "I am alone."

These names shape the reality we actualize. They are not neutral descriptions; they are creative acts that bring certain potentials into being and suppress others.

If you name an experience as "bad," you actualize its badness. You close yourself to any good that might be present in it. You position yourself as a victim of circumstances rather than a participant in reality.

If you name a person as "selfish," you actualize their selfishness. You will notice every action that confirms your naming and overlook actions that contradict it. You will relate to them as selfish, and they will likely respond in kind, creating a self-fulfilling prophecy.

This is not to say we should engage in positive thinking or denial, pretending that bad things are good or that selfish people are generous. That would be dishonest witnessing, a refusal to see what is there.

But it is to say that we must name with care, with awareness of the creative power of naming. We must ask: Is this name true? Is it complete? Does it actualize the reality I want to participate in creating?

Sometimes the most honest name is "I don't know." Sometimes the most creative name is a question rather than a statement.

The ball in the darkness might be blue. But it might also be more than blue—it might have textures, patterns, depths that the simple name "blue" does not capture. If we name it too quickly, too definitively, we might miss its fullness.

Conscious witnessing requires holding our names lightly, remaining open to renaming, to discovering new aspects of reality that our initial names did not capture.

WITNESSING WITH LOVE

Finally, and most importantly, conscious witnessing requires love. This might seem like a strange claim. What does love have to do with perception, with the actualization of reality?

Everything.

Love is the mode of consciousness that sees most truly, most completely. Not sentimental love, not romantic love, but the deep, abiding love that wills the good of the other, that desires to see the other as they truly are.

When you witness with love, you bring a quality of attention that is both focused and spacious. You notice details, but you also see the whole. You perceive flaws, but you also perceive beauty. You acknowledge suffering, but you also recognize dignity.

Love does not distort reality by seeing only the good. True love sees clearly—it sees the darkness as well as the light. But it sees the darkness in the context of the light, the brokenness in the context of the wholeness that is possible.

When you witness another person with love, you actualize their highest potential. You see not just who they are, but who they are becoming. You call forth the best in them through the quality of your attention.

This is what it means to be "seen" by someone who loves you. They do not ignore your flaws or pretend you are perfect. But they see you in your fullness, in your complexity, in your potential. And in being seen this way, you become more fully yourself.

The Architect witnesses us with love. This is the foundation of all reality. The universe exists because divine consciousness holds it in loving attention, actualizing its potential, calling it into being moment by moment.

And we are invited to participate in this loving witnessing. We are invited to see the world, and each other, and ourselves, with the same quality of attention that the Architect brings to us.

This is not easy. It requires practice, discipline, grace. It requires setting aside our fear, our judgment, our need to control. It requires vulnerability, openness, trust.

But it is the deepest calling of consciousness. It is what we were made for.

THE FLASHLIGHT IN YOUR HAND

Return one final time to the image of the sealed room, the darkness, the blue ball, the flashlight in your hand.

You now understand that turning on the flashlight is not a neutral act. It is a creative act, a participatory act. It will actualize a reality that does not exist in the darkness. You understand that how you shine the light matters. If you shine it carelessly, you will see only surfaces. If you shine it with attention, you will see depths. If you shine it with love, you will see truth.

You understand that you cannot not shine the light. To be conscious is to be a witness. The only question is whether you will be a conscious witness or an unconscious one.

The Architect has prepared this room. The Architect has placed the ball in the darkness. The Architect has given you the flashlight and invited you to turn it on.

This is not a burden, though it may feel like one. It is a gift. It is an invitation to participate in the most fundamental creative act in the universe: the actualization of reality through consciousness.

You are not alone in this room. The Architect is with you, witnessing your witnessing, holding you in the same loving attention that holds all of creation.

And beyond this room, there are other rooms, other witnesses, other balls waiting in other darknesses. We are all engaged in this work together, each actualizing our small portion of reality, each contributing to the great tapestry of existence.

The ball is waiting. The flashlight is in your hand. Turn on the light. See what is there. Name it with care. Witness it with love.

This is your calling. This is your gift. This is your participation in the eternal work of creation.

Pause here. Before moving to the next chapter, sit with what you have read. Notice what resonates and what resists. Notice what questions arise. Notice the quality of your own consciousness in this moment.

You are witnessing these words. But you are also witnessing your witnessing. You are conscious of being conscious.

This is the miracle. This is the mystery. This is the invitation.

What will you do with it?

THE SCRIPT OF THE BLOCK UNIVERSE

> "Before I formed you
> in the womb I knew you,
> before you were born
> I set you apart."
> — Jeremiah 1:5

The movie has already been filmed.

Every frame, from the opening credits to the final scene, exists simultaneously on the reel. The beginning, middle, and end are equally real, equally present, equally fixed. When you watch the movie, you experience it sequentially—one moment flowing into the next, the future unknown, the past receding behind you. But the movie itself does not unfold in time. It simply is, complete and unchanging.

You are a character in this movie. Your birth is a frame. Your death is a frame. Every choice you will ever make, every word you will ever speak, every thought you will ever think—all of it is already printed on the film.

This is the Block Universe.

It is one of the most unsettling ideas in physics and philosophy, and it is almost certainly true.

2.1 THE FILM THAT NEVER CHANGES

Let us begin with the physics, because the Block Universe is not merely a philosophical speculation. It is a consequence of our best scientific understanding of space and time.

EINSTEIN'S REVOLUTION

In 1905, Albert Einstein published his special theory of relativity, and the universe was never the same.

Before Einstein, we thought of space and time as separate, absolute, universal. Space was the stage on which events occurred. Time was the universal clock that ticked at the same rate for everyone, everywhere. The past was gone, the future had not yet arrived, and the present was a single, universal "now" that everyone shared.

Einstein showed that this picture is wrong.

Space and time are not separate; they are woven together into a single fabric called spacetime. And spacetime is not absolute; it is relative to the observer. Two observers moving at different speeds will disagree about the duration of events, the distance between objects, and even the order in which events occur.

Most radically, they will disagree about what "now" means.

Imagine two observers, Alice and Bob, separated by a great distance. Alice is on Earth; Bob is on a planet orbiting a star ten light-years away. If they are at rest relative to each other, they will agree on what is happening "now" on each other's planets—there is a shared present moment. But if Bob starts moving toward Alice at high speed, his "now" shifts. Events that were in Alice's future are suddenly in Bob's present. If Bob moves away from Alice, events that were in Alice's past are in Bob's present.

This is not an illusion or a trick of perception. It is a fundamental feature of spacetime. There is no universal "now." The present moment is relative to the observer.

And if the present is relative, then the distinction between past, present, and future is also relative. What is past for one observer may be present or future for another.

This leads to a startling conclusion: all moments in time must be equally real. The past has not ceased to exist; the future has not yet come into being. All moments exist simultaneously in the four-dimensional structure of spacetime.

This is the Block Universe.

THE GEOMETRY OF ETERNITY

Think of spacetime as a four-dimensional block, like a loaf of bread. Each slice of the bread represents a three-dimensional space at a particular moment in time. The entire loaf represents all of space at all moments in time. From our perspective, embedded within the block, we experience time as flowing. We move through the slices sequentially, experiencing one "now" after another. The past is the slices we have already passed through; the future is the slices we have not yet reached.

But from a perspective outside the block—a "God's eye view"—all the slices exist simultaneously. There is no flow, no becoming, no passage of time. There is only the complete, unchanging structure of spacetime, containing all events that ever were, are, or will be.

Your birth is a slice in this block. Your death is another slice. Every moment of your life is a slice. And all these slices exist together, eternally present in the four-dimensional geometry of spacetime.

This is not a metaphor. This is, according to our best physics, the actual structure of reality.

Einstein himself recognized the implications. In a letter written shortly after the death of his lifelong friend Michele Besso, Einstein wrote:

"Now he has departed from this strange world a little ahead of me. That means nothing. People like us, who believe in physics, know the distinction between past, present, and future is only a stubbornly persistent illusion." Only an illusion. The flow of time, the sense that the past is gone and the future is open—these are features of our subjective experience, not features of objective reality.

The movie has already been filmed. We are simply watching it unfold.

OBJECTIONS AND ALTERNATIVES

Before we explore the philosophical and theological implications, we should acknowledge that not all physicists accept the Block Universe.

Some argue for a "growing block" model, in which the past and present are real but the future is not yet determined. The block grows as time passes, adding new slices as events occur.

Others argue for "presentism," the view that only the present moment is real. The past has ceased to exist; the future does not yet exist. This view requires rejecting or reinterpreting relativity, which most physicists are unwilling to do.

Still others propose various forms of quantum mechanics that introduce genuine indeterminacy into the universe, suggesting that the future is not fixed but probabilistic. These are serious alternatives, and the debate continues. But the Block Universe remains the most straightforward interpretation of relativity, and it is the view held by many (perhaps most) physicists and philosophers of physics.

For our purposes, we will proceed with the Block Universe as our working model, while acknowledging that ultimate reality may be more complex or mysterious than any model can capture.

THE EXISTENTIAL SHOCK

If the Block Universe is true, then everything you will ever do is already determined. Not determined in the sense of being caused by prior events (though that may also be true), but determined in the sense of already existing in the four-dimensional structure of spacetime.

Your choices are already made. Your future is already written. The movie does not change.

This is deeply unsettling. It seems to rob life of meaning, to reduce us to puppets acting out a script we did not write and cannot alter.

But before we despair, we must examine this more carefully. We must ask: what does it mean to say the future is "already" determined? Already when? The word "already" implies a temporal sequence—first the future is undetermined, then it becomes determined. But in the Block Universe, there is no such sequence. All moments exist simultaneously. The future is not determined before it happens; it simply is, along with the past and present.

And we must ask: does the fixity of the future negate the reality of choice? Does the fact that your decisions are part of the unchanging structure of spacetime mean that you do not genuinely make those decisions?

These questions will occupy us for the rest of this chapter.

2.2 THE SENSATION OF FREEDOM WITHIN DETERMINISM

You feel free.

Right now, reading these words, you feel that you could stop reading if you chose to. You could close the book, stand up, walk away. The future feels open, full of possibilities, dependent on your choices.

This feeling is not an illusion, even if the Block Universe is true.

Let me say that again, because it is crucial: the sensation of freedom is real, even if the future is fixed.

COMPATIBILISM

In philosophy, there is a long tradition of "compatibilism"—the view that free will and determinism are compatible, that you can be genuinely free even if your actions are determined.

The key insight is that freedom is not the same as indeterminacy. Freedom is not the ability to have done otherwise in some absolute, metaphysical sense. Freedom is the ability to act according to your own desires, beliefs, and values, without external coercion.

When you choose to keep reading this book, that choice is free if it flows from your own curiosity, your own desire to understand, your own values. It does not matter whether that choice was determined by prior causes or whether it already exists in the Block Universe. What matters is that it is your choice, arising from who you are.

Contrast this with a choice made under coercion. If someone holds a gun to your head and demands that you keep reading, your choice is not free, even though it is still determined. The difference is not in the metaphysical status of the choice but in its relationship to your authentic self.

Freedom, in this view, is not about breaking the causal chain or escaping the Block Universe. It is about being the kind of being whose actions flow from internal deliberation, whose choices express genuine desires and values.

You are free when you are the author of your actions, even if the story you are authoring is already written.

THE PHENOMENOLOGY OF CHOICE

But this philosophical account, while logically coherent, may not fully satisfy. It does not capture the lived experience of choice, the felt sense of standing at a crossroads with multiple paths before you.

Let us examine this experience more carefully.

When you face a decision, you deliberate. You consider options, weigh pros and cons, imagine different futures. This deliberation feels meaningful. It feels like you are genuinely determining what will happen, not merely discovering what was always going to happen.

In the Block Universe, your deliberation is part of the determined structure. The fact that you deliberate, the considerations you weigh, the conclusion you reach—all of this is already part of the film.

But this does not make the deliberation meaningless. The deliberation is the mechanism by which the choice is made. It is not a separate process that could have led to a different outcome; it is the process that leads to the actual outcome. Think of it this way: the movie shows a character deliberating and then making a choice. The deliberation is part of the story. It is not external to the story, and it is not irrelevant to the story. It is how the character arrives at the choice that is already printed on the film.

From inside the movie, the character experiences the deliberation as genuine, the choice as open. From outside the movie, we see that the deliberation and choice are part of a fixed narrative.

Both perspectives are true. The character is genuinely deliberating and choosing. And the deliberation and choice are part of a predetermined story.

THE PARADOX OF FOREKNOWLEDGE

This brings us to an ancient theological puzzle: if God knows the future, how can we be free?

If God knows what you will choose before you choose it, then it seems your choice is not really free. You cannot choose otherwise than what God knows you will choose. Your future is fixed by divine foreknowledge.

But this puzzle rests on a confusion about time.

When we say God knows the future "before" it happens, we are thinking of God as existing in time, knowing future events from a temporal distance. But if God is eternal—existing outside of time, seeing all moments simultaneously—then God does not know the future before it happens. God simply knows it, in the eternal present that encompasses all of time.

In the Block Universe, this makes perfect sense. God sees the entire four-dimensional structure of spacetime at once. God sees your choice not before you make it, but in the eternal now that includes the moment of your choosing.

Your choice is free because it is genuinely yours, arising from your deliberation and your character. And your choice is known by God because God sees the entire structure of reality, including the moment when you freely choose.

There is no contradiction. Freedom and foreknowledge are compatible because they operate in different dimensions—freedom in the temporal experience of choice, foreknowledge in the eternal perspective that sees all of time at once.

THE WEIGHT OF RESPONSIBILITY

If the future is fixed, does that diminish moral responsibility?

Some people think so. They reason: if I could not have done otherwise, then I am not truly responsible for what I did. Responsibility requires the ability to have chosen differently. But this reasoning is flawed.

Responsibility does not require the metaphysical ability to have done otherwise. It requires that your action flow from your character, your values, your deliberation. It requires that you are the kind of being who can be held accountable, who can learn from consequences, who can be praised or blamed in ways that shape future behavior.

In the Block Universe, you are still this kind of being. Your choices are still yours. The fact that they are part of a fixed structure does not change their moral significance.

Consider: if you harm someone, the harm is real. The person suffers. You are the cause of that suffering. The fact that your action was determined, or that it already exists in the Block Universe, does not erase your responsibility for the harm.

Similarly, if you help someone, the help is real. The person benefits. You are the cause of that benefit. You deserve credit for your kindness, regardless of whether your action was determined.

Moral responsibility is about the relationship between your actions and their consequences, and about your capacity to respond to moral reasons. It is not about metaphysical indeterminacy. The movie may be fixed, but you are still responsible for your role in it.

THE DIGNITY OF PARTICIPATION

There is something profound about being a character in a story that is already written.

It means your life has a shape, a coherence, a meaning that transcends the moment-by-moment experience of living. Your life is not a random sequence of events; it is a narrative, with themes and patterns and purpose.

From inside the story, you experience uncertainty, possibility, choice. You do not know how the story will end. You must make decisions without knowing their full consequences.

But from outside the story—from the perspective of the Architect who sees the entire Block Universe—your life is a complete work, a finished creation. Every moment contributes to the whole. Every choice, every suffering, every joy is part of a larger pattern.

This does not diminish your agency. It elevates it. You are not merely reacting to random events; you are participating in a meaningful narrative. Your choices matter because they are part of the story, not in spite of being part of the story. Think of a great novel. The characters' choices are determined by the author, but they are not thereby rendered meaningless. The choices are what make the story compelling. The characters' agency is what gives the narrative its power.

You are a character in the greatest story ever told—the story of the universe itself, authored by the Architect. Your choices are real. Your freedom is real. And your life has a meaning and purpose that you are discovering as you live it, even though it has always been there, written into the structure of spacetime.

2.3 WHY THE MOVIE WATCHES YOU

We have established that the movie is fixed, that all moments exist simultaneously in the Block Universe. But there is a deeper mystery we must now confront: the movie is not merely a passive recording. It is alive. It is conscious. It is watching you even as you watch it.

This is where physics gives way to metaphysics, where science opens onto theology.

THE UNIVERSE AS CONSCIOUS

We have already explored the idea that consciousness actualizes reality, that the ball in the darkness becomes blue through the act of witnessing. But if the Block Universe is true, then all moments are equally real, including moments before human consciousness existed.

This suggests that consciousness is not merely a late-arriving feature of the universe, emerging after billions of years of unconscious evolution. Consciousness must be fundamental, woven into the fabric of reality from the beginning.

Some physicists and philosophers have proposed "panpsychism"—the view that consciousness is a basic property of matter, present at every level of reality. Electrons and quarks have some primitive form of experience; complex systems like brains have rich, integrated consciousness.

Others propose "idealism"—the view that consciousness is primary and matter is derivative, that the physical universe exists as an idea in the mind of God or as a structure within universal consciousness.

I am not committed to any particular metaphysical system. But I am committed to this: consciousness is not an accident. It is not a random byproduct of material complexity. It is essential to the nature of reality.

And if consciousness is essential, then the universe is not a dead mechanism. It is alive, aware, purposeful.

THE PARTICIPATORY UNIVERSE

The physicist John Wheeler proposed the idea of a "participatory universe"—a universe that requires observers to bring it into being.

Wheeler was thinking about quantum mechanics, where observation plays a crucial role in determining outcomes. But the idea extends beyond quantum mechanics to the very nature of reality.

In a participatory universe, observers are not external to reality, looking in from the outside. Observers are part of reality, and reality is incomplete without them.

The Block Universe contains all moments, including all moments of observation. Your consciousness, witnessing reality in this moment, is part of the Block. And the reality you witness is shaped by your witnessing, even though the witnessing is itself part of the predetermined structure.

This creates a kind of loop: reality shapes consciousness, and consciousness shapes reality. Neither is prior; both are mutually dependent.

The movie watches you because you are part of the movie. Your watching is part of what makes the movie what it is.

THE ARCHITECT'S PERSPECTIVE

Now we arrive at the theological heart of the matter. If the Block Universe is true, then the Architect sees all of time at once. The Architect does not experience temporal flow, does not wait for the future to arrive. The Architect sees your entire life—from birth to death, from first breath to last—in a single, eternal gaze.

This means the Architect knows you completely. Not just your actions, but your thoughts, your feelings, your struggles, your joys. Not just your present, but your past and your future. Not just what you show to the world, but what you hide even from yourself.

You are fully known.

This is terrifying. To be fully known is to be fully vulnerable, fully exposed. There is no hiding, no pretending, no managing your image. The Architect sees everything.

But it is also liberating. To be fully known is to be fully loved. The Architect does not love an idealized version of you or a partial version of you. The Architect loves the real you, the complete you, the you that exists across all of time in the Block Universe.

And the Architect has designed the universe—has written the movie—in such a way that you exist. Your life, with all its joys and sorrows, all its triumphs and failures, all its beauty and brokenness, is part of the intentional design. You are not an accident. You are not a random fluctuation in a meaningless cosmos. You are a character in a story authored by infinite love.

THE MOVIE CHANGES YOU

We said earlier that the movie does not change; the movie changes you.

This is the key to understanding the Block Universe from the inside.

Yes, the future is fixed. Yes, your choices are already part of the structure of spacetime. But you do not experience the future as fixed. You experience it as open, as dependent on your choices.

And in experiencing it this way, you are changed. Your character is formed through the process of deliberation and choice. Your identity is shaped by the narrative of your life.

The movie does not change because it is already complete. But you change because you are living through the movie, experiencing it sequentially, becoming who you are through the unfolding of the story.

Think of reading a novel for the second time. The story does not change—the words on the page are the same. But you change. You notice things you missed the first time. You understand characters differently. You see patterns and themes that were invisible before.

The novel is fixed, but your experience of the novel is dynamic.

Similarly, the Block Universe is fixed, but your experience of the Block Universe is dynamic. You are becoming who you are through the process of living, even though who you are is already written into the structure of spacetime.

THE ETERNAL SIGNIFICANCE OF TEMPORAL EXPERIENCE

This leads to a profound insight: your temporal experience has eternal significance.

The fact that you do not know the future, that you must make choices without certainty, that you experience suspense and surprise and discovery—all of this is not a bug in the system. It is a feature.

The Architect could have created beings who know the entire Block Universe, who see their lives from the outside as complete narratives. But such beings would not have the experience of becoming, of growth, of transformation through time.

You have been given the gift of temporal experience—the gift of living through the story rather than merely knowing it. And this gift is what makes you who you are. Your struggles are real, even though their outcome is already determined. Your choices are meaningful, even though they are already part of the Block. Your growth is genuine, even though the person you are becoming already exists in the future slices of spacetime.

The movie watches you because your experience of the movie is part of what makes the movie valuable. The Architect delights in your temporal journey, even though the Architect sees the journey as a complete whole.

You are not merely a character in a story. You are a character experiencing the story from the inside, and that experience is precious, irreplaceable, eternally significant.

2.4 LIVING INSIDE A FINISHED STORY

We have explored the metaphysics and theology of the Block Universe. Now we must ask the practical question: how should we live, knowing that the movie is already filmed?

Does the fixity of the future change how we should approach our choices, our relationships, our purpose?

THE TEMPTATION OF FATALISM

The first temptation is fatalism—the belief that because the future is fixed, our choices do not matter. "Why should I deliberate carefully about this decision? The outcome is already determined. Why should I work hard to achieve my goals? If I am meant to succeed, I will succeed; if I am meant to fail, I will fail. Why should I take responsibility for my actions? I am simply playing out a script I did not write."

This reasoning is seductive, but it is deeply flawed.

Your choices do matter, precisely because they are part of the determined structure. The future is fixed, but it is fixed in part by your choices. You are not external to the movie, watching it unfold. You are in the movie, and your choices are part of what makes the movie what it is.

If you choose not to deliberate carefully, that choice is part of the movie, and it will lead to certain consequences. If you choose not to work hard, that choice is part of the movie, and it will shape your future. If you choose to abdicate responsibility, that choice is part of the movie, and it will affect your character and your relationships.

The movie is fixed, but you are the one living it. Your experience, your growth, your becoming—these are real and valuable, regardless of whether they are predetermined. Fatalism is a refusal to participate fully in your own life. It is a form of spiritual laziness, a way of avoiding the hard work of choice and responsibility.

Do not fall into this trap.

THE PRACTICE OF PRESENCE

If the future is fixed, then every moment of your life already exists in the Block Universe. The moment you are experiencing right now is eternally present in the four-dimensional structure of spacetime.

This means that this moment matters. Not just as a stepping stone to some future moment, but in itself, as part of the eternal fabric of reality.

The practice of presence—of being fully attentive to the current moment—takes on new significance in the Block Universe.

When you are present, you are honoring the eternal reality of this moment. You are participating fully in the slice of spacetime that you currently inhabit. You are witnessing the world with the attention it deserves, actualizing the reality that is already there.

When you are distracted, lost in regret about the past or anxiety about the future, you are failing to honor the moment. You are sleepwalking through a slice of eternity. The past is not gone; it exists eternally in the Block. The future is not yet to come; it exists eternally in the Block. But you can only experience one slice at a time, and the slice you are experiencing is this one, now.

Give this moment the reverence it deserves.

THE PARADOX OF ETERNAL SIGNIFICANCE

Here is where the Block Universe becomes not a prison, but a cathedral.

If every moment exists eternally, then every moment of your life has eternal significance. The conversation you had this morning, the meal you ate, the kindness you showed or withheld—these are not fleeting events that disappear into nothingness. They are permanent features of the four-dimensional structure of reality.

Your life is not a series of moments that vanish as soon as they pass. Your life is a complete, eternal object in spacetime, as real and permanent as a mountain or a star.

This should change how you live.

When you understand that your actions are eternally inscribed in the fabric of reality, you begin to take them more seriously. Not out of fear, but out of reverence. You are not just living your life; you are creating an eternal artifact, a permanent contribution to the structure of the cosmos.

The Block Universe does not diminish the significance of your choices. It magnifies them infinitely.

Every act of love, every moment of courage, every instance of integrity—these are not temporary ripples that fade away. They are eternal truths, woven permanently into the tapestry of spacetime.

And every act of cruelty, every moment of cowardice, every betrayal—these too are permanent. Not as condemnations, but as part of the complete story of who you are and who you are becoming.

The Block Universe is not a judgment. It is a mirror. It shows you the eternal reality of your life, the permanent shape of your existence.

What will that shape be?

LIVING AS THOUGH THE STORY MATTERS

We have explored the metaphysics of the Block Universe, the paradox of freedom within determinism, the eternal significance of temporal experience. Now we must ask: how do we live in light of this understanding?

First, we live with intention. If the story is already written, then the story that is written is the story of your intentions, your values, your character. The predetermined nature of reality does not excuse you from responsibility; it reveals the eternal truth of who you are.

Live as though your choices matter, because they do. Not because they could have been otherwise, but because they are the authentic expression of your consciousness, your values, your deepest self.

Second, we live with presence. The Block Universe teaches us that every moment is eternally real, eternally significant. Do not waste your moments wishing you were somewhere else, someone else. You are here, now, in this slice of spacetime, and this moment will never come again—not because it passes away, but because you will never experience it again from this particular perspective.

Honor the moment by being fully present to it.

Third, we live with humility. The Block Universe reminds us that we are not the authors of reality. We are characters in a story that is larger than ourselves, a story that was complete before we became aware of it. This should inspire not despair, but wonder. You are part of something vast, something eternal, something infinitely more complex and beautiful than you can comprehend. Your role is not to control the story, but to participate in it fully, authentically, courageously.

Fourth, we live with hope. The Block Universe does not tell us what the future holds, only that it already exists. But from within the movie, the future is still unknown to us. We still experience surprise, discovery, transformation. The fact that these experiences are predetermined does not make them any less real or any less meaningful.

Hope is not the belief that the future is undecided. Hope is the trust that the future, whatever it holds, is part of a larger pattern, a deeper purpose, a story that makes sense even when we cannot see the whole.

And finally, we live with love. Love is the force that binds the Block Universe together, the thread that runs through every moment of spacetime. Love is what makes the predetermined story worth telling, worth experiencing, worth being.

When you love, you are participating in the deepest truth of reality. You are aligning yourself with the fundamental structure of the cosmos. You are becoming who you were always meant to be.

The movie does not change. But the movie is a love story, and you are in it.

THE WATCHER AND THE WATCHED

Before we leave the Block Universe, we must address one final question: who is watching the movie?

We have said that you are a character in the film, experiencing the story from within. But there is another sense in which you are also the audience, watching your own life unfold.

This is the mystery of self-awareness. You are not just living your life; you are witnessing it. You are both the actor and the observer, both the subject and the object of your own consciousness.

This dual nature of consciousness—the ability to be both participant and witness—is what makes spiritual growth possible. You can observe your own thoughts, your own emotions, your own behaviors. You can reflect on your life, learn from your experiences, change your patterns.

But here is the deeper truth: you are not the only one watching.

The Architect, who exists outside the Block, sees the entire film at once. Every moment of your life, from beginning to end, is visible to the divine gaze. You are not just watching yourself; you are being watched.

This is not surveillance. This is love. The Architect watches your life the way you might watch a beloved film, with complete attention, with deep investment, with intimate knowledge of every scene. The Architect knows you better than you know yourself, because the Architect sees the whole story, not just the slice you are currently experiencing.

And the Architect is not a passive observer. The Architect is the author, the director, the one who designed the story to teach you, to shape you, to bring you home.

The Block Universe is not a prison. It is a gift. It is the structure within which your consciousness can grow, your character can develop, your relationship with the Architect can deepen.

The movie is fixed, but the movie is also sacred. Every frame is intentional. Every moment is meaningful. Every experience is designed to teach you something essential about yourself, about reality, about the nature of love.

You are living inside a finished story, but it is a story written by infinite wisdom and infinite love. Trust the story. Trust the Architect. Trust that even the difficult scenes, the painful moments, the confusing chapters—all of it is part of a larger pattern that you will one day understand. The lights are on. The movie is playing. You are both the character and the witness.

What will you see?

Pause here. Before moving to the next chapter, sit with the paradox of the Block Universe. You are free and you are determined. Your choices matter and they are already made. You are living in time and you exist in eternity.

Can you hold both truths at once?

This is the beginning of wisdom.

THE HIDDEN VARIABLE

> "Nothing in all creation
> is hidden from God's sight.
> Everything is uncovered and laid bare
> before the eyes of him to whom
> we must give account."
>
> — Hebrews 4:13

There is a box in your mind.

You have been filling it for as long as you can remember. Into this box go all the things you do not want others to see: the shameful thoughts, the secret desires, the moments of weakness, the calculated deceptions, the small cruelties, the hidden fears.

You believe this box is sealed. You believe its contents are yours alone, locked away from the world, safe from judgment and exposure. You are wrong. The box does not exist.

Or rather, it exists only as a psychological construct, a comforting fiction that allows you to maintain the illusion of privacy in a universe where nothing is truly hidden.

This chapter is about the collapse of that illusion. It is about what happens when you realize that the Architect sees everything—not as a violation of your privacy, but as the fundamental condition of existence.

It is about the terror and the freedom of being completely known.

3.1 THE ILLUSION OF SECRETS

THE ARCHITECTURE OF CONCEALMENT

Human beings are masters of concealment. We learn early in life that there are things we must hide: our vulnerabilities, our desires, our true thoughts and feelings. We learn to wear masks, to perform roles, to present carefully curated versions of ourselves to the world.

This is not entirely bad. Some degree of privacy is necessary for psychological health. We need boundaries, spaces where we can be ourselves without constant scrutiny or judgment. But somewhere along the way, concealment becomes more than a practical necessity. It becomes a way of life. We begin to believe that our true selves must be hidden, that if others saw us as we really are, they would reject us, condemn us, abandon us.

And so we build the box. We create elaborate systems of secrecy, layers of protection around our inner lives. We tell ourselves that what others don't know can't hurt us.

But the box is not just about protecting ourselves from others. It is also about protecting ourselves from ourselves.

When we hide our shame, our fear, our darkness in the box, we do not have to confront it. We do not have to acknowledge it, process it, integrate it. We can pretend it does not exist, or at least that it is not really part of who we are.

The box allows us to maintain a false image of ourselves—not just to others, but to ourselves. It is the foundation of self-deception.

THE METAPHYSICS OF HIDING

But let us think more carefully about what it means to hide something. When you hide an object in the physical world, you are placing it somewhere that is difficult for others to access. You are creating a barrier between the object and potential observers. The object still exists, but it is obscured from view.

This works because physical objects exist in space, and space can be divided, partitioned, blocked off. You can put something in a locked drawer, and as long as the drawer remains locked, the object is hidden.

But thoughts are not physical objects. Memories are not stored in locked drawers. Your inner life does not exist in a private space that can be sealed off from observation.

Your consciousness is not a container. It is a process, a dynamic flow of experience that arises in relationship with the world. And that relationship is not private. It is embedded in the larger fabric of reality, the Block Universe we explored in the previous chapter.

Every thought you have, every feeling you experience, every intention you form—these are events in spacetime. They are part of the four-dimensional structure of reality. They exist, eternally, in the Block.

And the Architect, who exists outside the Block, sees all of it. Not because the Architect is spying on you, but because the Architect is the ground of reality itself. The Architect is not an external observer peering into your private space. The Architect is the condition of possibility for your existence. You exist in the Architect, and the Architect exists in you.

There is no box. There never was.

THE PSYCHOLOGY OF EXPOSURE

The realization that you cannot hide from the Architect is terrifying.

We have built our entire psychological lives around the assumption that we can control what others know about us. We have invested enormous energy in managing our image, protecting our secrets, maintaining our masks.

And now we are being told that it was all for nothing. That the Architect has seen everything all along. That every shameful thought, every secret sin, every hidden fear has been completely visible from the beginning.

This feels like a violation. It feels like an invasion of privacy, an assault on our autonomy, a stripping away of our defenses.

But consider: what if the Architect's knowledge of you is not a violation, but a form of intimacy? What if being fully known is not something to fear, but something to desire?

Think about the relationships in your life where you feel most loved, most accepted, most at home. These are not the relationships where you are most hidden. They are the relationships where you are most seen.

When someone truly knows you—knows your flaws, your struggles, your darkness—and loves you anyway, that is a profound gift. It is the opposite of violation. It is validation. It is the experience of being accepted not in spite of who you are, but because of who you are, in all your complexity and contradiction.

The Architect's knowledge of you is like this, but infinitely more complete. The Architect knows you better than you know yourself. The Architect sees not just your actions, but your intentions. Not just your words, but your heart. Not just your present, but your past and your future, your potential and your limitations, your wounds and your gifts.

And the Architect loves you.

Not the carefully curated version of yourself that you present to the world. Not the idealized self you wish you were. But the real you, the complete you, the you that exists in the Block Universe in all your messy, complicated, beautiful reality.

This is the terror and the freedom of being fully known.

THE ETHICS OF TRANSPARENCY

If you cannot hide from the Architect, what does this mean for how you live?

First, it means that your ethical life cannot be based on avoiding detection. You cannot be good only when others are watching, because you are always being watched. The Architect sees not just your public actions, but your private thoughts, your secret motivations, your hidden intentions.

This might sound oppressive, like living under constant surveillance. But consider the alternative: an ethics based on appearance rather than reality, on performance rather than authenticity, on managing your image rather than cultivating your character.

When you know you are always seen, you are freed from the exhausting work of maintaining a false front. You can stop performing and start being. You can align your inner life with your outer life, your private self with your public self.

This is integrity in the deepest sense: wholeness, integration, the unity of self that comes from living transparently. Second, it means that your relationship with the Architect must be based on honesty. You cannot manipulate God. You cannot hide your true self and present a sanitized version for divine approval. The Architect already knows everything. The only question is whether you will acknowledge it.

This is what confession is really about. Not informing God of something God doesn't already know, but aligning your conscious awareness with the reality that God already sees. It is the practice of bringing what is hidden into the light, not to create knowledge, but to create honesty.

When you confess, you are not revealing yourself to God. You are revealing yourself to yourself. You are acknowledging the truth that has always been visible to the divine gaze.

Third, it means that your spiritual growth depends on your willingness to be known. As long as you are hiding, you cannot grow. As long as you are maintaining the illusion of the box, you cannot integrate the parts of yourself that you have locked away.

Spiritual maturation requires radical honesty—with yourself, with others, and with the Architect. It requires the courage to let the box be opened, to let the light shine on everything you have tried to hide.

This is painful. It is humbling. It is terrifying. But it is also liberating.

THE PRACTICE OF HONESTY

How do we live in light of the truth that we cannot hide?

We begin by practicing honesty in our relationship with ourselves. We stop pretending that the box is sealed. We acknowledge that the things we have hidden are still part of us, still shaping our thoughts and behaviors, still demanding our attention.

This might mean journaling, therapy, meditation, or simply quiet reflection. It means creating space to look at the contents of the box without judgment, without shame, without the need to immediately fix or change what we find.

It means saying to ourselves: "This is also me. This darkness, this fear, this shame—it is part of my story, part of my humanity, part of what I am learning to integrate and transform."

We continue by practicing honesty in our relationships with others. We take small risks of vulnerability, sharing parts of ourselves that we usually keep hidden. We let people see us more fully, trusting that true intimacy requires true knowledge.

This does not mean oversharing or violating appropriate boundaries. It means being authentic, being real, being willing to be known rather than always managing how we are perceived.

And we deepen the practice by cultivating honesty in our relationship with the Architect. We pray not with carefully crafted words designed to impress, but with raw honesty about our struggles, our doubts, our failures, our fears.

We stop trying to be the person we think God wants us to be, and we start being the person we actually are, trusting that the Architect already knows us completely and loves us anyway.

This is the beginning of spiritual freedom: the recognition that you have nothing to hide because you cannot hide anything, and that this is not a curse but a blessing.

The box is an illusion. Let it go.

3.2 DIVINE OMNISCIENCE AND HUMAN VULNERABILITY

THE NATURE OF DIVINE KNOWLEDGE

When we say that the Architect knows everything, what exactly do we mean?

In classical theology, divine omniscience is often described as God's knowledge of all true propositions. God knows every fact, every event, every thought, every possibility. God's knowledge is complete, perfect, and eternal.

But this abstract definition does not capture the full reality of what it means to be known by God.

The Architect's knowledge is not like a database, a collection of information stored and retrieved. It is not like surveillance, an external observation of your behavior. It is not even like mind-reading, an intrusion into your private thoughts.

The Architect's knowledge is more intimate than any of these metaphors suggest.

Remember the Block Universe. All of reality—past, present, and future—exists eternally in the four-dimensional structure of spacetime. The Architect, existing outside this structure, sees it all at once, in a single eternal present.

This means the Architect does not just know about you. The Architect knows you, in the most complete sense possible. The Architect knows you from the inside, as it were, because you exist within the divine consciousness.

Your existence is not separate from God's existence. You are not an independent entity that God observes from a distance. You are a manifestation of divine creativity, a particular expression of the infinite consciousness that grounds all reality.

When the Architect knows you, it is not like one person knowing another person. It is like the ocean knowing a wave, like a tree knowing a branch, like consciousness knowing a thought.

You are not hidden from God because you cannot be separated from God. Your existence is held within the divine existence. Your consciousness arises within the divine consciousness.

This is why the box is an illusion. There is no private space where you can hide from God, because there is no space that is not already within God.

THE VULNERABILITY OF BEING KNOWN

To be completely known is to be completely vulnerable.

Vulnerability is the state of being open to harm, to judgment, to rejection. When we are vulnerable, we have no defenses, no protections, no masks. We are exposed, naked, defenseless.

This is why we build the box. Vulnerability is terrifying. It feels dangerous. We believe that if we are fully seen, we will be fully rejected.

But here is the paradox: true intimacy requires vulnerability. True love requires being known. Think about the relationships in your life. The ones that feel most superficial are the ones where you are most defended, most hidden, most protected. You interact with these people from behind your masks, sharing only what is safe, revealing only what is acceptable.

These relationships are comfortable, but they are not intimate. They do not touch the deepest parts of you. They do not satisfy your longing to be truly known and truly loved.

The relationships that matter most are the ones where you have risked vulnerability. Where you have let someone see your weakness, your fear, your shame. Where you have been honest about who you really are, not just who you wish you were.

And when that vulnerability is met with acceptance, with compassion, with love—that is when you experience true connection. That is when you feel most fully alive, most fully yourself, most fully at home in the world.

The Architect offers you this kind of relationship, but at an infinite scale.

The Architect sees you completely—more completely than you see yourself, more completely than anyone else could ever see you. The Architect sees your past and your future, your conscious thoughts and your unconscious motivations, your greatest achievements and your deepest failures.

And the Architect loves you.

Not in spite of what the Architect sees, but including what the Architect sees. The Architect's love is not conditional on your goodness, your success, your worthiness. The Architect's love is the ground of your existence, the reason you are here at all.

You are vulnerable before God, completely and eternally. But this vulnerability is not a threat. It is an invitation to intimacy, to the deepest relationship possible, to the experience of being fully known and fully loved.

THE FEAR OF JUDGMENT

But what about judgment?

If the Architect sees everything, including our sins, our failures, our darkness, doesn't that mean we will be judged? Doesn't that mean we should be afraid?

This is a legitimate fear, and we must take it seriously.

The biblical tradition is clear that there is such a thing as divine judgment. We are accountable for our actions. Our choices have consequences. The way we live matters, not just to us, but to the Architect who created us and loves us. But judgment is not the same as condemnation.

Judgment, in its truest sense, is the act of seeing clearly, of discerning truth from falsehood, of recognizing what is real. When the Architect judges you, the Architect is simply seeing you as you are, without illusion, without distortion, without the masks and defenses you use to hide from yourself.

This kind of judgment is not punitive. It is revelatory. It shows you the truth about yourself, the truth you have been avoiding or denying or hiding in the box.

And yes, this truth can be painful. It can be humbling. It can shatter your self-image and force you to confront parts of yourself you would rather ignore.

But this pain is not punishment. It is medicine. It is the pain of healing, the pain of growth, the pain of becoming more fully yourself.

The Architect's judgment is always in service of love. The Architect sees your darkness not to condemn you, but to heal you. The Architect exposes your secrets not to shame you, but to free you from the burden of hiding.

Think of it this way: a doctor who examines you and finds a disease is not punishing you by making the diagnosis. The doctor is helping you by revealing what needs to be healed. The diagnosis might be frightening, but it is also the first step toward health. The Architect's judgment is like this. It is diagnostic, not punitive. It reveals what needs to be healed so that healing can begin.

And the Architect does not just diagnose. The Architect also heals. The same divine knowledge that sees your wounds is also the divine love that binds them up.

You are seen, and you are loved. You are judged, and you are forgiven. You are known completely, and you are accepted completely.

This is grace.

THE FREEDOM OF TRANSPARENCY

When you stop trying to hide from the Architect, something remarkable happens: you become free.

The energy you were spending on concealment, on maintaining the box, on managing your image—all of that energy is suddenly available for other purposes. You can use it to grow, to love, to create, to become more fully yourself.

You no longer have to worry about being found out, because there is nothing to find out. Everything is already known. You no longer have to fear exposure, because you are already fully exposed. You no longer have to perform, because the Architect sees past all performances to the reality beneath. This is the freedom of transparency: the freedom to be yourself, completely and without reservation.

It is the freedom to fail without shame, because the Architect already knows your failures and loves you anyway.

It is the freedom to be weak without pretense, because the Architect already knows your weaknesses and offers you strength.

It is the freedom to be honest without fear, because the Architect already knows your truth and invites you to live in it.

This freedom does not mean you can do whatever you want without consequences. Your actions still matter. Your choices still shape your character and your relationships. The Block Universe is still fixed, and your life is still part of that eternal structure.

But you are free from the exhausting work of hiding. You are free from the prison of self-deception. You are free from the fear that if people really knew you, they would reject you.

Because the one who really knows you—who knows you better than anyone, who knows you completely and eternally—does not reject you. The Architect embraces you, holds you, loves you with an infinite and unconditional love.

This is the freedom that comes from being fully known.

THE PRACTICE OF VULNERABILITY

How do we cultivate this kind of transparency in our lives?

We begin by practicing vulnerability with ourselves. We stop hiding from our own consciousness. We look honestly at our thoughts, our feelings, our motivations, our fears. We acknowledge what is really there, not what we wish were there.

This might mean sitting in meditation and observing your thoughts without judgment. It might mean journaling about your struggles without censoring yourself. It might mean simply pausing throughout the day and asking yourself: "What am I really feeling right now? What am I really afraid of? What am I really wanting?"

We continue by practicing vulnerability with others. We take small risks of honesty in our relationships. We share something real, something that matters, something that makes us feel exposed.

This does not mean dumping all your problems on everyone you meet. It means being authentic in your interactions, letting people see the real you rather than the performed you. It means saying "I don't know" when you don't know, rather than pretending to have all the answers. It means admitting when you're struggling, rather than always projecting strength. It means asking for help when you need it, rather than maintaining the illusion of self-sufficiency.

And we deepen the practice by cultivating vulnerability with the Architect. We pray with radical honesty. We bring our doubts, our anger, our confusion, our darkness into our relationship with God.

We stop trying to be the perfect spiritual person and start being the real person we are, trusting that the Architect already knows us completely and invites us into deeper intimacy, not despite our imperfections, but through them.

This is the spiritual practice of transparency: learning to live as though you are fully known, because you are.

The box is an illusion. The secrets are already revealed. The only question is whether you will acknowledge this truth and live in the freedom it offers.

3.3 THE BEGINNING OF WISDOM

THE FEAR OF THE LORD

The biblical tradition speaks often of "the fear of the Lord" as the beginning of wisdom. This phrase troubles many modern readers. Why should we fear a God who loves us? Isn't fear the opposite of love? Doesn't perfect love cast out fear?

But the fear spoken of here is not terror. It is not the fear of punishment or condemnation. It is something deeper, something more fundamental.

The fear of the Lord is the recognition of reality.

It is the acknowledgment that you are not the center of the universe, that you are not the author of reality, that you are not in control. It is the recognition that you exist within a larger order, a cosmic structure that you did not create and cannot manipulate.

It is the recognition that you are seen.

This recognition is the beginning of wisdom because it is the beginning of truth. As long as you believe you can hide, you are living in illusion. As long as you believe you can control how you are perceived, you are living in fantasy. As long as you believe the box is real, you are living in self-deception.

The fear of the Lord shatters these illusions. It confronts you with the reality that you are completely known, completely visible, completely transparent to the divine gaze. And this confrontation is terrifying—not because God is cruel, but because truth is always terrifying to those who have been living in lies.

But on the other side of this terror is freedom. On the other side of this fear is wisdom. On the other side of this confrontation with reality is the possibility of living in truth.

THE COLLAPSE OF SELF-DECEPTION

Self-deception is one of the most powerful forces in human psychology. We are remarkably skilled at lying to ourselves, at constructing narratives that protect our self-image, at avoiding truths that threaten our sense of identity.

We tell ourselves we are good people, even as we act selfishly. We tell ourselves we are victims, even as we harm others. We tell ourselves we are in control, even as our lives spiral into chaos.

These lies are not usually conscious. We do not deliberately deceive ourselves. Rather, we construct elaborate psychological defenses that prevent us from seeing what is really there.

The box is part of this system of self-deception. By hiding our darkness from ourselves, we can maintain the illusion that we are better than we are, that we are not responsible for our failures, that we are not complicit in our own suffering.

But the recognition that we cannot hide from the Architect collapses this system.

If the Architect sees everything, then the Architect sees through our self-deceptions. The Architect knows the truth we are hiding from ourselves. The Architect sees the gap between who we pretend to be and who we really are.

And because the Architect sees this truth, we can no longer avoid it. We can no longer maintain the comfortable lies we tell ourselves. We are confronted with reality, whether we like it or not.

This is painful. It is humbling. It can feel like a kind of death—the death of the false self, the death of the illusions we have built our lives around.

But it is also the beginning of wisdom.

Because wisdom is not about knowing more things. Wisdom is about seeing clearly. It is about perceiving reality as it is, not as we wish it were. It is about living in truth rather than in fantasy.

And you cannot live in truth as long as you are deceiving yourself.

You cannot see clearly as long as you are hiding from what is really there. The fear of the Lord—the recognition that you are completely known—forces you to confront the truth about yourself. It strips away your defenses, your illusions, your comfortable lies.

And in that stripping away, wisdom becomes possible.

THE GIFT OF BEING KNOWN

We have spoken of the terror of being fully known, the vulnerability it requires, the self-deception it exposes. But we must also speak of the gift.

To be fully known is to be fully loved.

This is the deepest longing of the human heart: to be seen completely and accepted completely, to be known in all our complexity and loved in all our imperfection.

We spend our lives seeking this kind of love. We long for relationships where we can be ourselves, where we don't have to perform or pretend, where we can be vulnerable without fear of rejection.

But human relationships, no matter how deep, can never fully satisfy this longing. No human being can know you completely. No human being can see all of you—your past and your future, your conscious and unconscious, your potential and your limitations. And even if they could, human love is always conditional to some degree. It is shaped by the other person's needs, their wounds, their limitations. It can be withdrawn, betrayed, lost.

But the Architect's knowledge is complete, and the Architect's love is unconditional.

The Architect sees you more fully than you see yourself. The Architect knows your deepest secrets, your darkest thoughts, your most shameful moments. The Architect knows every failure, every weakness, every time you have fallen short.

And the Architect loves you.

Not in spite of what the Architect sees, but including what the Architect sees. The Architect's love is not based on your performance, your worthiness, your goodness. It is based on the simple fact that you exist, that you are a beloved creation, that you are held eternally in the divine consciousness.

This is the gift of being known: the experience of unconditional love, the love that sees everything and accepts everything, the love that knows you completely and embraces you completely.

This is what your soul has been longing for all along.

THE TRANSFORMATION OF SHAME

Shame is the feeling that there is something fundamentally wrong with you, something that makes you unworthy of love and belonging. Shame is not about what you have done; it is about who you are.

Shame thrives in secrecy. It grows in the darkness of the box, feeding on the belief that if others knew the truth about you, they would reject you. Shame tells you that you must hide, that you must keep your darkness secret, that you must never let anyone see the real you.

But the recognition that you cannot hide from the Architect transforms shame.

If the Architect sees everything—including the things you are most ashamed of—and still loves you, then shame loses its power. The thing you were most afraid of—being fully known—has already happened. And you have not been rejected. You have been embraced.

This does not mean your shame disappears immediately. Shame is a deep wound, and healing takes time. But the recognition that you are fully known and fully loved begins the process of healing.

You no longer have to carry your shame in secret. You can bring it into the light, into the presence of the Architect who already knows it and loves you anyway.

You can begin to see your shame not as evidence of your unworthiness, but as a wound that needs healing, a part of your story that needs integration, a teacher that has something to show you about your humanity.

And as you bring your shame into the light, it begins to transform. It loses its power to control you, to define you, to keep you trapped in hiding.

This is the alchemy of grace: the transformation of shame into humility, of hiding into honesty, of self-rejection into self-acceptance.

THE PRACTICE OF WISDOM

Wisdom begins with the fear of the Lord—the recognition that you are fully known. But wisdom does not end there. Wisdom is a practice, a way of living, a continual orientation toward truth.

How do we cultivate wisdom in our daily lives?

We begin by practicing honesty. We stop lying to ourselves about who we are, what we want, what we fear. We look at reality as it is, not as we wish it were.

This means paying attention to our thoughts, our feelings, our behaviors. It means noticing when we are deceiving ourselves, when we are avoiding uncomfortable truths, when we are constructing narratives that protect our ego rather than revealing reality. It means asking ourselves hard questions: Why did I really do that? What am I really afraid of? What am I really avoiding? What truth am I not willing to see?

We continue by seeking feedback from others. We ask people we trust to tell us the truth about ourselves, even when that truth is difficult to hear. We listen to criticism without immediately defending ourselves. We consider the possibility that others might see things about us that we cannot see ourselves.

This requires humility—the recognition that we do not have perfect self-knowledge, that we are prone to self-deception, that we need others to help us see clearly.

We deepen the practice by cultivating a relationship with the Architect based on honesty rather than performance. We pray not to impress God, but to align ourselves with the truth that God already sees.

We confess not to inform God of our sins, but to acknowledge them ourselves, to bring them into the light, to stop hiding from what is already known.

We ask not for God to change reality, but for the wisdom to see reality clearly and the courage to live in alignment with it.

And we practice discernment—the ability to distinguish truth from falsehood, reality from illusion, wisdom from foolishness. We test our thoughts and beliefs against reality. We notice when our narratives do not match our experience. We remain open to being wrong, to learning, to growing.

Wisdom is not a destination. It is a journey, a continual practice of seeing more clearly, living more honestly, aligning more fully with the truth of who we are and who the Architect is calling us to become.

THE INVITATION TO TRUTH

We have explored the illusion of secrets, the vulnerability of being known, the transformation that comes from living in truth. Now we must ask: will you accept the invitation?

The Architect is inviting you to step out of hiding. To let the box be opened. To live in the light of truth rather than in the darkness of self-deception.

This invitation is not a demand. The Architect does not force you to be honest. You are free to continue hiding, to continue maintaining your illusions, to continue living in the comfortable lies you tell yourself.

But you should know: the hiding is exhausting. The illusions are fragile. The lies are ultimately unsustainable. And on the other side of hiding is freedom. On the other side of illusion is reality. On the other side of lies is the truth that will set you free.

The Architect already knows you completely. The only question is whether you will acknowledge this truth and live in the freedom it offers.

Will you let yourself be known? Will you step into the light? Will you accept the gift of being seen and loved, completely and eternally?

This is the beginning of wisdom: the recognition that you cannot hide, and the acceptance that you do not need to.

The box is an illusion.

Let it go.

Pause here. Before moving to the next chapter, consider: what are you hiding? What secrets are you keeping in the box? What would it mean to bring them into the light?

The Architect already knows. The only question is whether you will acknowledge what is already known.

This is the invitation to wisdom. Will you accept it?

PART II

THE CLASSROOM AND ITS LESSONS

—

GRADUATION AND THE GREATER DESTINATION

"For now we see through a glass, darkly; but then face to face: now I know in part; but then shall I know even as also I am known."

— 1 Corinthians 13:12

Imagine a child in school.

The child sits at a desk, learning to read, to write, to calculate. The child struggles with difficult concepts, makes mistakes, experiences frustration and occasional triumph. The child does not always understand why these lessons matter, why this particular curriculum has been chosen, why some things are easy and others are impossibly hard.

But the child trusts—or at least hopes—that there is a purpose to it all. That the teacher knows something the child does not. That these lessons are preparing the child for something larger, something beyond the classroom.

And one day, the child graduates. The child leaves the classroom and enters the wider world, where the lessons learned suddenly make sense in ways they never did before. The abstract concepts become practical tools. The difficult exercises become useful skills. The whole curriculum reveals itself as preparation for a life the child could not have imagined while sitting at that desk.

This is the metaphor we will explore in this chapter: the universe as a classroom, and you as a student preparing for graduation.

But graduation from what? And into what?

4.1 THE UNIVERSE AS TEMPORARY STRUCTURE

THE SCAFFOLDING OF REALITY

When a building is under construction, it is surrounded by scaffolding—temporary structures that support the work of building but are not part of the final structure. The scaffolding is essential during construction, but once the building is complete, the scaffolding is removed.

The physical universe is like scaffolding.

This is a startling claim, and it contradicts our usual assumptions about reality. We tend to think of the physical world as the most real thing there is, the solid foundation upon which everything else rests.

But what if the physical world is not the foundation? What if it is the scaffolding? What if matter, energy, space, and time are temporary structures—essential for a particular phase of development, but not the ultimate reality?

This is what the great spiritual traditions have always taught. The physical world is maya, illusion, a veil that obscures deeper truth. The material realm is a shadow of the eternal realm, a temporary manifestation of something more fundamental.

But we must be careful here. To say that the physical world is temporary is not to say it is unimportant. The scaffolding is essential during construction. Without it, the building cannot be built.

Similarly, the physical universe is essential for the development of consciousness, for the formation of souls, for the teaching of lessons that can only be learned through embodied experience.

The universe is not a mistake or a prison or a punishment. It is a classroom, carefully designed by the Architect to teach you what you need to learn.

But it is temporary. It is scaffolding. And one day, when the building is complete, the scaffolding will be removed.

THE TESTIMONY OF PHYSICS

Remarkably, modern physics supports this view. We know that the universe had a beginning—the Big Bang, approximately 13.8 billion years ago. Before that moment, there was no space, no time, no matter, no energy. The physical universe came into existence at a specific point.

And we know that the universe will have an end. The second law of thermodynamics tells us that entropy—disorder—is always increasing. Eventually, all the stars will burn out, all the black holes will evaporate, all the energy will be evenly distributed, and the universe will reach a state of maximum entropy called heat death.

At that point, no further change will be possible. No life, no consciousness, no experience. Just an infinite, cold, dark, empty expanse.

This is the fate of the physical universe according to our best scientific understanding. The scaffolding will eventually collapse.

But here is the question: if the physical universe is temporary, what is permanent?

The answer, according to the spiritual traditions, is consciousness. The witness. The soul. The relationship between the individual mind and the Architect.

These are not physical things. They do not depend on matter or energy for their existence. They are not subject to entropy or heat death. They are eternal.

The physical universe is the classroom where consciousness develops, where souls are formed, where the relationship with the Architect is established. But the classroom is not the destination. The classroom is preparation for something beyond itself.

THE PURPOSE OF LIMITATION

If the physical universe is temporary scaffolding, why does it exist at all? Why did the Architect create this elaborate structure if it is just going to be dismantled?

The answer is that the limitations of the physical world serve a purpose.

In the physical world, you are constrained. You have a body that gets tired, hungry, sick. You have a mind that forgets, makes mistakes, struggles to understand. You exist in time, which means you experience change, loss, mortality. You exist in space, which means you are separated from others, isolated in your own perspective.

These limitations are not accidents. They are features of the classroom, designed to teach you specific lessons.

The limitation of the body teaches you about vulnerability, dependence, the need for care and rest. It teaches you that you are not self-sufficient, that you need others, that you are part of a larger web of life.

The limitation of the mind teaches you humility. It shows you that you do not know everything, that you are prone to error, that you need to remain open to learning and growth.

The limitation of time teaches you about change, about the preciousness of each moment, about the reality of loss and the hope of renewal. It teaches you that nothing in the physical world lasts forever, that you must hold things lightly, that you must learn to let go.

The limitation of space teaches you about otherness, about the existence of perspectives different from your own, about the challenge and gift of relationship. It teaches you that you are not alone, that you are not the center of the universe, that you are part of a community of consciousness.

These limitations are the curriculum of the classroom. They are what make learning possible.

In an unlimited existence—where you could do anything, know anything, be anything—there would be nothing to learn. There would be no growth, no development, no transformation.

But in a limited existence, you are forced to confront your finitude, your dependence, your need for something beyond yourself. You are forced to grow, to adapt, to learn.

The limitations of the physical world are not punishments. They are pedagogical tools, carefully calibrated to teach you what you need to learn.

THE ILLUSION OF PERMANENCE

One of the most important lessons the classroom teaches is that nothing physical is permanent.

We resist this lesson. We cling to the illusion that the things we love will last forever, that the structures we build will endure, that we ourselves will not die.

But the physical world is constantly teaching us otherwise. Everything changes. Everything decays. Everything ends.

Your body ages. Your relationships evolve. Your possessions break or wear out. The institutions you trust crumble. The certainties you relied on dissolve.

This is not a flaw in the design of the universe. This is the design of the universe.

The impermanence of the physical world is meant to teach you not to place your ultimate trust in physical things. It is meant to turn your attention toward what is permanent: the eternal relationship with the Architect, the consciousness that transcends the physical, the love that endures beyond death.

When you cling to the physical as though it were permanent, you are setting yourself up for suffering. You are investing your hope in something that is designed to be temporary, like building your house on sand.

But when you recognize the temporary nature of the physical world, you can hold it more lightly. You can appreciate it without clinging to it. You can love it without being destroyed by its loss.

This is one of the central lessons of the classroom: learn to distinguish between the temporary and the eternal, between the scaffolding and the building, between the classroom and the destination.

THE PRACTICE OF DETACHMENT

How do we live in light of the temporary nature of the physical world?

We practice detachment—not as indifference or coldness, but as a form of wisdom.

Detachment does not mean you stop caring about the physical world. It does not mean you stop loving people, stop enjoying beauty, stop working to make the world better. Detachment means you hold these things with an open hand rather than a clenched fist. It means you appreciate them without clinging to them. It means you recognize their temporary nature and love them anyway, knowing that their impermanence is part of their beauty.

Think of a sunset. You do not try to hold onto the sunset, to freeze it in place, to prevent it from fading. You appreciate it precisely because it is fleeting. Its temporary nature is part of what makes it precious.

This is how we are meant to relate to all physical things: with appreciation, with gratitude, with love—but also with the recognition that they are temporary, that they are part of the scaffolding, that they are not the ultimate reality.

We practice detachment by noticing when we are clinging. When we are anxious about losing something, when we are desperate to control an outcome, when we are devastated by change—these are signs that we are clinging to the temporary as though it were permanent.

In these moments, we can pause and ask ourselves: What am I really afraid of losing? What am I trying to hold onto? What would it mean to hold this more lightly? We practice detachment by cultivating gratitude for what is present without demanding that it last forever. We enjoy the meal without needing to eat it again tomorrow. We appreciate the conversation without needing to repeat it. We love the person without needing to possess them.

And we practice detachment by investing our deepest hope not in the physical world, but in the eternal reality that transcends it. We place our trust not in the scaffolding, but in the building. Not in the classroom, but in the destination.

This is the wisdom of recognizing the temporary nature of the physical world: it frees us to love the world more fully, because we are no longer terrified of losing it.

4.2 WHAT GRACE TEACHES

THE CENTRAL CURRICULUM

If the universe is a classroom, what is the lesson?

We have spoken of many lessons: humility, vulnerability, detachment, the distinction between temporary and eternal. But there is one lesson that stands at the center of the curriculum, the lesson that all other lessons serve.

That lesson is grace. Grace is the unmerited love of the Architect. It is the gift that cannot be earned, the love that is not based on your worthiness, the acceptance that is not conditional on your performance.

Grace is the fundamental truth of your relationship with the Architect: you are loved not because of what you do, but because of who you are. You are loved not because you are good, but because you are.

This is the hardest lesson to learn, because it contradicts everything the world teaches you.

The world teaches you that love must be earned. That you must prove your worth. That you must perform, achieve, succeed in order to be accepted.

The world teaches you that you are only as valuable as your productivity, your beauty, your intelligence, your accomplishments. That if you fail, if you fall short, if you reveal your weakness, you will be rejected.

And so you spend your life trying to earn love, trying to prove your worth, trying to be good enough to deserve acceptance.

But grace says: you cannot earn it. You do not need to earn it. It is already yours. This is almost impossible to believe. It seems too good to be true. It seems to violate the basic logic of the universe, the principle that you get what you deserve.

But grace is not about what you deserve. Grace is about what the Architect freely gives.

And the classroom of the universe is designed to teach you this truth, over and over, in a thousand different ways.

THE PEDAGOGY OF FAILURE

One of the primary ways the classroom teaches grace is through failure.

When you fail—when you make a mistake, when you fall short, when you reveal your weakness—you are confronted with a choice.

You can interpret your failure as evidence of your unworthiness. You can use it to confirm your deepest fear: that you are not good enough, that you do not deserve love, that you should be rejected.

Or you can interpret your failure as an opportunity to experience grace. You can use it to discover that you are loved even in your failure, that your worth is not based on your performance, that the Architect's acceptance is not conditional on your success. This is why failure is such an important part of the curriculum. It is the laboratory where grace is tested and proven.

When you succeed, it is easy to believe you are loved because you are worthy. When you fail, you discover whether you are loved regardless of your worthiness.

And the testimony of countless souls who have walked this path is clear: the Architect's love does not waver in the face of your failure. The Architect does not withdraw, does not condemn, does not reject.

The Architect meets you in your failure with compassion, with patience, with the invitation to try again, to learn, to grow.

This is grace: the love that does not depend on your success.

THE PEDAGOGY OF SUFFERING

Another way the classroom teaches grace is through suffering.

Suffering strips away your illusions of self-sufficiency. It reveals your vulnerability, your dependence, your need for something beyond yourself.

When you are suffering, you cannot pretend to be in control. You cannot maintain the illusion that you are strong enough, smart enough, good enough to handle everything on your own.

Suffering breaks you open. It exposes your need. It forces you to reach out, to ask for help, to acknowledge your dependence on others and on the Architect.

And in that moment of vulnerability, you become capable of receiving grace.

As long as you believe you can earn love through your own efforts, you do not need grace. You do not need a gift; you believe you can pay for what you need.

But when suffering reveals that you cannot pay, that you do not have the resources to save yourself, that you are utterly dependent on something beyond yourself—then you become open to receiving the gift.

This is not to say that suffering is good in itself. Suffering is real, and it is painful, and we should work to alleviate it wherever we can.

But suffering can serve a pedagogical purpose. It can teach you what comfort cannot teach: that you are not self-sufficient, that you need grace, that the Architect's love is not something you earn but something you receive.

We will explore this more deeply in the next chapter. For now, it is enough to recognize that suffering is part of the curriculum, and that one of its purposes is to open you to the experience of grace.

THE PEDAGOGY OF LOVE

The classroom also teaches grace through love—both the love you receive and the love you give.

When you experience being loved by another person—truly loved, not for what you do but for who you are—you get a glimpse of grace. You experience what it is like to be accepted without having to earn it, to be valued without having to prove your worth.

This human love is imperfect, of course. It is limited by the other person's capacity, their wounds, their needs. It can be withdrawn or betrayed.

But even imperfect human love points toward the perfect love of the Architect. It gives you a taste of what it means to be loved unconditionally, to be accepted completely, to be valued infinitely.

And when you love another person—when you choose to accept them without demanding that they earn your love, when you value them for who they are rather than what they do—you are participating in grace. You are embodying the Architect's love. You are becoming a channel through which grace flows into the world. This is one of the most profound lessons of the classroom: you learn grace not just by receiving it, but by giving it. You understand the Architect's love more deeply when you practice loving others the way the Architect loves you.

THE PEDAGOGY OF FORGIVENESS

Perhaps the most powerful way the classroom teaches grace is through forgiveness.

When you are wronged—when someone hurts you, betrays you, fails you—you are faced with a choice.

You can hold onto the wrong. You can nurse your grievance, demand justice, insist that the other person pay for what they have done.

Or you can forgive. You can release the debt, let go of the demand for payment, offer the wrongdoer a grace they do not deserve.

Forgiveness is costly. It requires you to absorb the pain of the wrong rather than passing it back to the wrongdoer. It requires you to give up your right to revenge, to restitution, to seeing the other person suffer as you have suffered.

But forgiveness is also liberating. It frees you from the prison of resentment, from the exhausting work of keeping score, from the bitterness that poisons your own soul.

And forgiveness is the clearest expression of grace. When you forgive, you are doing for another what the Architect does for you: offering love that is not earned, acceptance that is not deserved, a fresh start that is pure gift. The classroom teaches you to forgive by putting you in situations where you are wronged. It gives you opportunities to practice grace, to embody the love you have received, to become more like the Architect.

And the classroom also teaches you to receive forgiveness—to acknowledge your own wrongs, to accept the grace that is offered to you, to let yourself be loved even when you do not deserve it.

Both giving and receiving forgiveness are essential parts of the curriculum. Both teach you what grace is and how it works.

THE PRACTICE OF RECEIVING

How do we learn the lesson of grace?

We begin by practicing receiving.

This is harder than it sounds. We are trained to be self-sufficient, to earn what we get, to pay our own way. We are uncomfortable with gifts, especially gifts we have not earned. But grace is a gift. It cannot be earned. It can only be received.

So we practice receiving. We practice accepting help when it is offered. We practice saying thank you without immediately trying to repay the favor. We practice letting ourselves be loved without feeling like we have to earn it.

We practice receiving forgiveness when we have wronged someone. We practice accepting that we are loved even in our failure. We practice trusting that the Architect's acceptance is not conditional on our performance.

This requires humility—the recognition that we are not self-sufficient, that we need grace, that we cannot save ourselves.

And it requires trust—the belief that the Architect's love is real, that it is offered freely, that it will not be withdrawn when we fail.

We continue by practicing giving. We practice offering grace to others—forgiving when we are wronged, loving when it is not earned, accepting people as they are rather than demanding that they change.

When we give grace, we understand it more deeply. We experience the cost of it, the freedom of it, the transformative power of it. And we deepen the practice by paying attention to the ways the classroom is teaching us grace. We notice when failure opens us to receiving love we have not earned. We notice when suffering reveals our dependence on something beyond ourselves. We notice when forgiveness frees us from the prison of resentment.

The classroom is always teaching. The question is whether we are paying attention.

4.3 BEYOND THE BLOCK

THE LIMITS OF SPACETIME

We have explored the Block Universe—the four-dimensional structure of spacetime in which all moments exist eternally. We have seen how this framework helps us understand the relationship between freedom and determinism, between temporal experience and eternal reality.

But the Block Universe is not the final word. It is not the ultimate reality. It is part of the scaffolding, part of the classroom.

The Block Universe is the structure of the physical world, the framework within which matter and energy and consciousness interact. But it is a limited structure. It is bounded by the beginning and end of the physical universe. It is subject to the laws of physics, the constraints of spacetime.

And beyond the Block lies something else. Something that transcends the physical, that is not subject to the limitations of spacetime, that is not part of the temporary scaffolding.

What is this something else?

The spiritual traditions have many names for it: eternity, the eternal realm, the kingdom of God, nirvana, the Absolute, the One.

We will call it simply: the Beyond.

THE NATURE OF THE BEYOND

The Beyond is not a place. It is not located in space or time. It is not part of the physical universe.

The Beyond is the eternal reality that grounds the physical universe, the permanent structure that the temporary scaffolding supports, the destination that the classroom prepares you for.

In the Beyond, there is no time. Not in the sense that time is frozen, but in the sense that time is transcended. Past, present, and future do not exist as separate moments. There is only the eternal now, the infinite present. In the Beyond, there is no space. Not in the sense that everything is compressed into a point, but in the sense that space is transcended. There is no separation, no distance, no isolation. There is only unity, connection, communion.

In the Beyond, there is no matter. Not in the sense that everything is empty, but in the sense that matter is transcended. There is only consciousness, spirit, the direct presence of the Architect.

This is almost impossible to imagine from within the classroom. We are so embedded in spacetime, so accustomed to thinking in terms of past and future, here and there, self and other, that we cannot conceive of a reality that transcends these categories.

But the spiritual traditions testify that such a reality exists, and that it is more real, more fundamental, more true than the physical world we experience.

The physical world is a shadow of the Beyond. The Block Universe is a reflection of eternity. The classroom is a preparation for the destination.

THE RELATIONSHIP BETWEEN BLOCK AND BEYOND

How do the Block Universe and the Beyond relate to each other? One way to think about it is that the Block Universe exists within the Beyond, the way a thought exists within a mind.

The Architect, who exists in the Beyond, creates the Block Universe as a temporary structure, a classroom for the development of consciousness. The entire four-dimensional spacetime—from the Big Bang to the heat death of the universe—exists as a complete object within the eternal consciousness of the Architect.

From the perspective of the Beyond, the Block Universe is already complete. It has already happened, in a sense, because in eternity there is no "not yet." The entire story is present to the Architect in a single eternal now.

But from within the Block, we experience the story sequentially.

We move through time, experiencing one moment after another, living the story from the inside.

This dual perspective—the eternal view from the Beyond and the temporal view from within the Block—is essential to understanding the purpose of the classroom.

The classroom exists in time so that you can experience growth, change, development. You cannot learn without time, because learning is a process that unfolds sequentially. But the destination exists in eternity, where all learning is complete, all growth is fulfilled, all development is realized.

The classroom prepares you for the destination. The Block prepares you for the Beyond.

GRADUATION

What does it mean to graduate from the classroom?

In the metaphor, graduation is the moment when you leave the temporary structure of the physical world and enter the eternal reality of the Beyond.

In traditional religious language, this is often called death, resurrection, salvation, enlightenment, liberation.

But we must be careful not to think of graduation as simply the end of physical life. Graduation is not just about dying. It is about transformation, about becoming ready for the Beyond.

You can begin graduating while you are still in the classroom. You can begin to live in the reality of the Beyond even while you are still embodied in the physical world.

This is what the spiritual traditions call awakening, enlightenment, union with God. It is the experience of transcending the limitations of the physical world while still inhabiting it, of touching eternity while still living in time.

When you awaken, you begin to see the classroom for what it is: a temporary structure designed to teach you grace. You begin to see the physical world as scaffolding rather than foundation. You begin to orient yourself toward the Beyond rather than clinging to the Block.

This does not mean you abandon the physical world. You are still in the classroom, still learning the lessons, still participating in the curriculum.

But you are no longer trapped by the illusion that the physical world is all there is. You are no longer terrified of losing what is temporary. You are no longer investing your ultimate hope in the scaffolding.

You are beginning to live in the reality of the Beyond, even while you are still in the classroom.

THE PROMISE OF DIRECT KNOWLEDGE

One of the most profound differences between the classroom and the destination is the nature of knowledge.

In the classroom, your knowledge is always partial, always mediated, always indirect. You know things through your senses, through your reasoning, through the testimony of others. You see through a glass, darkly.

But in the Beyond, knowledge is direct. You do not know about the Architect; you know the Architect. You do not know about reality; you are united with reality. You do not see through a glass; you see face to face.

This is the promise of graduation: the end of all mediation, all separation, all mystery.

In the classroom, you are always at a distance from what you seek to know. There is always a gap between the knower and the known, between your consciousness and the reality you are trying to understand.

But in the Beyond, this gap collapses. You know even as you are known. You are united with the Architect in a relationship of perfect intimacy, perfect transparency, perfect love.

This is what the soul longs for: not just to know about God, but to know God. Not just to understand truth, but to be united with truth.

Not just to experience love, but to be love.

The classroom prepares you for this union. It teaches you grace so that you can receive the infinite love of the Architect. It teaches you humility so that you can surrender your illusion of self-sufficiency. It teaches you detachment so that you can let go of the temporary and embrace the eternal.

And when you are ready—when the lessons are learned, when the curriculum is complete, when the building is finished—the scaffolding is removed, and you enter the Beyond.

THE PRACTICE OF ANTICIPATION

How do we live in light of the Beyond?

We practice anticipation—not as escapism or wishful thinking, but as a form of orientation.

Anticipation means living with the awareness that the classroom is not the destination. It means holding the physical world lightly, knowing that it is temporary. It means investing your deepest hope not in what is passing away, but in what is eternal.

This does not mean you stop caring about the physical world. It does not mean you stop working to make the world better, stop loving people, stop engaging with the challenges of embodied life.

It means you do these things with a different spirit. You do them as a student in a classroom, learning the lessons, practicing the skills, preparing for graduation.

You love people not as possessions to be clung to, but as fellow students on the journey. You work for justice not as the ultimate goal, but as practice in embodying grace. You appreciate beauty not as something to be preserved forever, but as a glimpse of the eternal beauty that awaits in the Beyond.

We practice anticipation by cultivating desire for the Beyond. We allow ourselves to long for the direct knowledge of the Architect, for the end of separation, for the perfect love that casts out all fear.

This longing is not a rejection of the present. It is a recognition that the present is not all there is, that you were made for something more, that the classroom is preparation for a destination that exceeds your wildest imagination.

And we practice anticipation by living as though the Beyond is already breaking into the present. We practice seeing the eternal in the temporal, the sacred in the ordinary, the presence of the Architect in the midst of the physical world.

The Beyond is not just a future destination. It is the eternal reality that grounds the present moment. When you learn to see it, you discover that you are already living in the presence of what you seek.

The classroom is not separate from the destination. It is the path that leads there. And the path is already sacred, already infused with the presence of the Architect, already teaching you what you need to know.

Pause here. Before moving to the next chapter, consider: What is the classroom teaching you right now? What lessons are you learning? What is preparing you for the Beyond?

The universe is not random. It is not meaningless. It is a carefully designed curriculum, teaching you grace, preparing you for graduation.

Are you paying attention?

Are you learning the lessons?

Are you ready for what comes next?

THE ETERNAL REWARD

"And this is eternal life, that they know you,
the only true God, and Jesus Christ
whom you have sent."

— John 17:3

What do you want?

This is not a trivial question. It is perhaps the most important question you will ever answer. What do you want, in the deepest part of yourself? What are you seeking? What are you longing for? What would satisfy the hunger in your soul?

Many people answer this question with a list of things: wealth, success, pleasure, security, recognition, power.

But if you are honest, you know that these things do not satisfy. You have pursued them, perhaps achieved them, and discovered that they leave you still hungry, still seeking, still longing for something more.

What you really want—what every human soul really wants—is not a thing. It is a relationship.

You want to be known and to be loved. You want to know and to love. You want to be connected, to belong, to be at home in the universe.

You want the Architect.

This chapter is about the eternal reward: not a prize you win for good behavior, but the relationship you were created for, the destination the classroom has been preparing you for, the fulfillment of your deepest longing.

5.1 TRUTH AS PERSON, NOT FORMULA

THE LIMITS OF ABSTRACTION

Throughout this book, we have explored abstract concepts: consciousness, the Block Universe, divine omniscience, grace, the Beyond.

These concepts are useful. They help us think clearly about reality. They give us frameworks for understanding our experience.

But there is a danger in abstraction. The danger is that we begin to think of truth as a set of propositions, a collection of correct ideas, a formula we can master.

We begin to think that if we just understand the right concepts, if we just believe the right doctrines, if we just grasp the right philosophy, we will have arrived at truth.

But truth is not a formula. Truth is a person.

This is one of the most radical claims of the Christian tradition, and it is easy to miss its significance. When Jesus says, "I am the way, the truth, and the life," he is not claiming to teach the truth. He is claiming to be the truth.

Truth is not an abstract principle. Truth is the Architect, the divine consciousness that grounds all reality, the infinite love that creates and sustains the universe.

And you cannot have a relationship with an abstraction. You cannot love a formula. You cannot be known by a concept. You can only have a relationship with a person.

THE PERSONAL NATURE OF REALITY

This is a startling claim, and it contradicts much of modern thinking.

We are trained to think of reality as impersonal, as a collection of physical laws and mathematical relationships that operate mechanically, without intention or purpose.

We are trained to think of truth as objective, as something that exists independently of any consciousness, as a set of facts that are true whether anyone believes them or not.

And in one sense, this is correct. The physical laws do operate consistently. The facts are what they are, regardless of our beliefs.

But this impersonal view of reality is incomplete. It describes the scaffolding, but it misses the Architect. It describes the classroom, but it misses the Teacher.

At the foundation of reality is not a law or a principle or a formula. At the foundation of reality is a consciousness, a will, a love.

The Architect is not an impersonal force. The Architect is a person—not in the sense of having a physical body, but in the sense of having consciousness, intention, the capacity for relationship.

And this changes everything.

If reality is ultimately impersonal, then your existence is an accident, your consciousness is a fluke, your longing for meaning is a cruel joke. You are alone in an indifferent universe, and your life has no ultimate significance beyond the brief flicker of your biological existence.

But if reality is ultimately personal—if the Architect is conscious, intentional, relational—then your existence is meaningful. Your consciousness is a gift. Your longing for connection is a response to the One who longs for you.

You are not alone. You have never been alone. And your life has eternal significance because you are known and loved by the consciousness that grounds all being.

This is the eternal reward: not a place, not a state, but a relationship. The direct, unmediated knowledge of the Architect, and the Architect's direct, unmediated knowledge of you.

THE LIMITS OF METAPHOR

Throughout this book, we have used metaphors to approach these truths: the void and the witness, the block universe and the movie, the classroom and graduation, the box and the hidden variable.

These metaphors are necessary because we are finite beings trying to grasp infinite realities. We see through a glass, darkly. We cannot comprehend the fullness of the Architect's nature or the complete structure of reality.

But metaphors have limits. They illuminate certain aspects of truth while obscuring others. They help us understand, but they can also mislead if we mistake the map for the territory.

The danger is that we become attached to our metaphors, that we confuse our conceptual frameworks with the reality they attempt to describe. We build theological systems, philosophical arguments, doctrinal statements—and we forget that these are all fingers pointing at the moon, not the moon itself.

The eternal reward is not a concept to be grasped intellectually. It is a person to be known relationally.

You cannot arrive at the Architect through logic alone, though logic can clear away obstacles. You cannot reach the Architect through ritual alone, though ritual can create space for encounter. You cannot find the Architect through morality alone, though morality can align you with the Architect's nature. The Architect is found through relationship. Through opening yourself to the presence that has always been there. Through recognizing that you are already known, already seen, already loved.

This is why the great mystics across traditions speak of unknowing, of darkness, of silence. Not because the Architect is absent, but because the Architect exceeds all our categories, transcends all our concepts, surpasses all our language.

The eternal reward is the dissolution of the distance between knower and known. It is the recognition that you have always existed within the consciousness of the Architect, that your life has always been held within the eternal love that creates and sustains all things.

THE JOURNEY TOWARD PERSON

How do we move from abstract understanding to personal encounter? How do we shift from knowing about the Architect to knowing the Architect?

This is the work of a lifetime, and it cannot be reduced to a formula. But there are practices, disciplines, orientations that can open us to the possibility of encounter.

First, we must cultivate honesty. We must be willing to see ourselves as we truly are—not the carefully curated self we present to others, but the full reality of our thoughts, desires, fears, and longings. This is the wisdom we explored in Chapter 3: the recognition that we cannot hide from the Architect, and therefore we need not hide from ourselves.

Second, we must cultivate humility. We must recognize the limits of our understanding, the partiality of our perspective, the incompleteness of our knowledge. This creates space for revelation, for the possibility that reality is larger and stranger and more beautiful than we have imagined.

Third, we must cultivate attention. We must learn to be present to the moment, to notice what is actually here rather than being lost in abstraction or distraction. This is the practice we will explore more fully in Chapter 8: the discipline of witnessing with full consciousness.

Fourth, we must cultivate openness. We must be willing to be surprised, to have our assumptions challenged, to discover that the Architect is not who we thought. This requires letting go of our need to control, our demand for certainty, our insistence that reality conform to our expectations.

And finally, we must cultivate desire. We must allow ourselves to want the Architect, to long for the relationship that is our deepest purpose. This desire is not something we manufacture; it is something we uncover, something that has always been there beneath the layers of distraction and defense.

These practices do not earn the Architect's love. They do not make us worthy of relationship. They simply remove the obstacles we have placed between ourselves and the presence that has always been seeking us.

The Architect is already here. The Architect has always been here. The question is whether we are willing to turn and see.

5.2 THE INTENTIONAL UNIVERSE

THE QUESTION OF PURPOSE

We have established that the Architect is personal, that reality is grounded in consciousness and relationship rather than impersonal mechanism. But this raises a profound question: Why?

Why does the universe exist at all? Why did the Architect create the Block Universe, the classroom of space and time, the scaffolding of matter and energy?

This is the question of purpose, and it is one of the deepest questions we can ask. It is also one of the most difficult to answer, because it requires us to speculate about the intentions of a consciousness infinitely greater than our own. But we are not without clues. The structure of reality itself reveals something about the Architect's purposes. The nature of our experience points toward the reasons for our existence.

Let us begin with what we can observe: the universe is structured to produce consciousness. The physical constants are fine-tuned to allow for the emergence of complex structures—stars, planets, molecules, cells, brains. The laws of physics permit the development of systems that can process information, respond to their environment, and eventually become aware of their own awareness.

This is sometimes called the anthropic principle: the observation that the universe appears to be calibrated for the existence of observers. Change any of the fundamental constants by even a tiny amount, and you get a universe that cannot support life, let alone consciousness.

Some argue this is simply selection bias—of course we find ourselves in a universe that permits our existence, because we couldn't exist in any other kind of universe. This is true as far as it goes, but it doesn't explain why there is a universe at all, or why it has the particular structure it does.

The intentional interpretation is that the universe is designed to produce consciousness because consciousness is the point. The Architect creates a reality that can give rise to beings capable of awareness, relationship, and eventually reunion with their source.

THE LOGIC OF LOVE

But why would the Architect desire this? What purpose does it serve for an infinite, eternal, self-sufficient consciousness to create finite, temporal, dependent beings?

Here we must tread carefully, because we are attempting to understand motivations that transcend our categories. But there is a logic to love that may illuminate the question.

Love, by its nature, desires relationship. Love seeks to share itself, to communicate itself, to create space for the beloved to exist and flourish. Love is not content to remain alone; it overflows, it gives, it creates.

This is not because love is incomplete or lacking. The Architect does not need us in the way we need food or air or shelter. The Architect's existence is not diminished by our absence or enhanced by our presence.

But love, even when complete in itself, desires to share its completeness. Love wants the beloved to experience the joy, the beauty, the goodness that love knows. Love creates not out of necessity but out of abundance.

Think of an artist who creates not because they lack something, but because they are full of vision and want to express it. Think of a parent who has a child not to fill a void, but to share the gift of existence. Think of a teacher who instructs not for personal gain, but for the joy of seeing understanding dawn in another's mind.

The Architect creates because love creates. The universe exists because the Architect desires to share existence with beings capable of receiving it, experiencing it, and ultimately returning it in relationship.

This is why consciousness is central to the design. Unconscious matter can exist, but it cannot know that it exists. It cannot experience beauty or meaning or love. It cannot enter into relationship with its creator.

But conscious beings can. We can know that we exist. We can wonder about our existence. We can ask why we are here and what our purpose is. We can seek the Architect and, in seeking, begin to find.

THE GIFT OF OTHERNESS

For relationship to be real, there must be genuine otherness. The beloved must be truly other than the lover, must have their own existence, their own perspective, their own capacity to respond or refuse.

This is why the universe is structured as it is—with space that creates distance, time that creates sequence, matter that creates boundaries. These limitations are not flaws in the design; they are necessary conditions for the existence of beings who are genuinely other than the Architect.

If we were simply extensions of the Architect's consciousness, there would be no real relationship. There would be no dialogue, no discovery, no possibility of genuine encounter. We would be like the Architect's thoughts—part of the Architect's own mental life rather than separate beings capable of knowing and being known.

But the universe creates the conditions for genuine otherness. You are not the Architect. You have your own perspective, your own experience, your own consciousness. You can choose to seek the Architect or turn away. You can open yourself to relationship or close yourself off.

This otherness is a gift, even though it comes with the possibility of separation, loneliness, and suffering. It is what makes relationship possible. It is what makes love real rather than merely self-love reflected back. The Block Universe, with all its determinism, still preserves this otherness. Yes, your choices are part of the predetermined structure. But they are still your choices, arising from your character, your desires, your understanding. The movie is written, but you are genuinely a character in it, not merely a puppet.

And the Architect, who exists beyond the Block, encounters you as genuinely other. The Architect knows you completely, but this knowledge is relational, not merely informational. It is the knowledge of love, which sees and affirms the beloved in their full reality.

THE PURPOSE OF THE CLASSROOM

We have described the universe as a classroom, a temporary structure designed to teach certain lessons. But now we can be more specific about what those lessons are for.

The classroom exists to prepare us for relationship with the Architect.

Think about what relationship requires: the capacity to see and be seen, to know and be known, to give and receive, to trust and be trustworthy. These capacities do not emerge automatically. They must be developed, practiced, refined.

The universe provides the conditions for this development. Through our relationships with other beings, we learn what it means to encounter genuine otherness. Through our experiences of beauty, we develop the capacity for wonder and appreciation. Through our struggles with limitation, we learn humility and dependence.

Through suffering—and we will explore this more fully in the next chapter—we learn compassion, depth, and the difference between shallow happiness and deep joy. Through moral choice, we develop character and learn to align our will with what is good and true.

All of these lessons prepare us for the eternal reward: direct, unmediated relationship with the Architect. They develop in us the capacities we will need to receive and respond to the infinite love that is our ultimate destination.

This is why the classroom is temporary. It is not the destination; it is the preparation for the destination. Once we have learned what we need to learn, once we have developed the capacities we need to develop, the scaffolding can be removed.

And what remains is relationship—the relationship that was always the point, the relationship for which we were created, the relationship that will fulfill every longing and answer every question.

THE INTENTIONALITY OF YOUR EXISTENCE

This means that your existence is not accidental. You are not a cosmic fluke, a random arrangement of atoms that happened to achieve self-awareness. You are intentional.

The Architect created the universe knowing that you would emerge from it. The Block Universe includes every moment of your life, from your first breath to your last, and the Architect sees it all in a single, eternal gaze.

You were created for relationship. Your consciousness, your capacity for awareness and wonder and love, is a gift designed to enable that relationship. Your life, with all its joys and sorrows, successes and failures, is part of the curriculum preparing you for your ultimate purpose.

This does not mean that everything that happens to you is directly willed by the Architect. The universe operates according to natural laws, and those laws produce both beauty and tragedy, both pleasure and pain. Other beings have their own agency, and their choices affect you in ways that may be harmful.

But it does mean that your existence as a whole is held within the Architect's intention. You are not forgotten, not overlooked, not insignificant. You are known, seen, loved, and called toward a destiny that exceeds anything you can imagine. This is the foundation of confidence, which we will explore in the next section. When you understand that you are intentional, that your existence has purpose, that you are moving toward a destination of infinite love and perfect knowledge, you can face the uncertainties and difficulties of life with courage and hope.

You are not alone in an indifferent universe. You are a beloved child of the Architect, learning what you need to learn, becoming who you need to become, moving toward the relationship for which you were created.

5.3 LIVING IN CONFIDENCE

THE NATURE OF CONFIDENCE

Confidence, in the deepest sense, is not the same as certainty. Certainty is the claim to possess complete knowledge, to have eliminated all doubt, to be absolutely sure of our beliefs and interpretations.

But confidence is different. Confidence is the ability to move forward in the face of uncertainty, to act with courage even when we cannot see the full picture, to trust that we are held even when we cannot prove it.

This distinction is crucial for spiritual seekers. We will never have certainty about the ultimate nature of reality. We see through a glass, darkly. Our knowledge is partial, our understanding incomplete, our metaphors imperfect. But we can have confidence. We can trust that the universe is intentional, that our existence has meaning, that we are moving toward a destination of love and knowledge. We can live as though we are seen and known and held, even when we cannot empirically verify it.

This confidence is not blind faith that ignores evidence or refuses to engage with doubt. It is a trust that emerges from paying attention to the structure of reality, the nature of consciousness, the depth of our longing, and the moments of encounter that hint at the presence of the Architect.

It is a confidence that can coexist with questions, with uncertainty, with the recognition that we might be wrong about many things. But it is also a confidence that allows us to commit, to orient our lives toward the Architect, to live as though the relationship we long for is real.

THE PRACTICE OF TRUST

How do we cultivate this confidence? How do we learn to trust when we cannot be certain?

First, we must recognize that trust is always a risk. There is no way to eliminate the possibility of being wrong, of being disappointed, of discovering that reality is other than we hoped. Trust requires vulnerability, the willingness to open ourselves to the possibility of both fulfillment and heartbreak.

But this risk is unavoidable. Even the decision not to trust is a kind of trust—trust that the universe is indifferent, that meaning is illusory, that we are ultimately alone. There is no neutral position, no way to avoid the fundamental choice about how we will orient ourselves toward reality.

Given this, the question becomes: which trust is more aligned with what we observe and experience? Which orientation toward reality makes better sense of consciousness, beauty, meaning, love, and the deep longing for connection that characterizes human existence?

The confidence we are describing is the trust that these things are not illusions, that they point toward something real, that the universe is structured to support relationship rather than to frustrate it.

This trust is strengthened through practice. We learn to trust by trusting, by taking small steps of faith and observing what happens. We orient ourselves toward the Architect and pay attention to how this orientation affects our experience, our relationships, our sense of meaning and purpose.

We practice honesty, allowing ourselves to be seen as we truly are. We practice humility, acknowledging the limits of our understanding. We practice attention, becoming present to the moment rather than lost in abstraction. We practice openness, allowing ourselves to be surprised by reality.

And as we practice these things, we often find that our confidence deepens. Not because we have achieved certainty, but because we have experienced moments of encounter, glimpses of the presence we seek, hints that we are indeed known and held and loved.

LIVING AS THOUGH YOU ARE SEEN

One of the most transformative practices is to live as though you are seen—not in the sense of being watched by a judgmental observer, but in the sense of being known by a loving presence.

We explored this in Chapter 3, when we discussed the impossibility of hiding from the Architect. But now we can approach it from a different angle: not as a threat to our privacy, but as an invitation to authenticity.

When you live as though you are seen, you no longer need to maintain the exhausting performance of pretending to be someone you're not. You can let go of the carefully curated self-image, the defensive postures, the strategies of concealment and control.

You can be yourself—fully, honestly, without reservation. Because you are already known, there is nothing to hide. Because you are already loved, there is nothing to prove.

This does not mean you become careless about your behavior or indifferent to how you affect others. On the contrary, living as though you are seen often makes us more thoughtful, more intentional, more aligned with our deepest values.

When you know you are seen, you become more conscious of your choices. You ask yourself: Is this who I want to be? Is this action aligned with my true self? Am I living in a way that honors the gift of existence?

But this self-examination is not driven by fear of punishment or desire for reward. It is driven by the desire to be authentic, to live in integrity, to align your outer life with your inner truth.

And paradoxically, this often makes us more compassionate toward ourselves. When we recognize that the Architect sees our struggles, our failures, our limitations, and loves us anyway, we can extend that same compassion to ourselves.

We can acknowledge our mistakes without being crushed by shame. We can recognize our limitations without being paralyzed by inadequacy. We can accept ourselves as we are while still growing toward who we are becoming.

THE CONFIDENCE TO ACT

Living in confidence also means having the courage to act, to make choices, to commit to a path even when we cannot see the full destination.

Many spiritual seekers become paralyzed by uncertainty. They want to be absolutely sure before they commit, to have all their questions answered before they take a step. But this kind of certainty is not available to finite beings living in time.

Confidence allows us to act in the face of uncertainty. It allows us to say: I do not know everything, but I know enough to take the next step. I cannot see the full picture, but I can see what is in front of me. I cannot prove that I am right, but I can trust that I am held.

This confidence is especially important when it comes to moral action. We often face situations where the right choice is unclear, where competing values create genuine dilemmas, where we must act without knowing all the consequences.

Living in confidence means trusting that we can make the best choice we can with the information we have, and that the Architect holds us even when we make mistakes. It means recognizing that moral growth happens through practice, through trial and error, through learning from our failures as well as our successes. It also means trusting that our actions matter, that our choices have significance, that we are participating in something larger than ourselves. Even though the Block Universe is predetermined, even though the movie is already written, our choices are real and meaningful. They shape who we become, they affect others, they contribute to the unfolding of the story.

THE CONFIDENCE TO REST

Finally, living in confidence means having the freedom to rest, to let go of the need to control everything, to trust that we are held even when we are not striving.

Much of our anxiety comes from the belief that everything depends on us, that if we do not maintain constant vigilance and effort, everything will fall apart. We carry the weight of the world on our shoulders, terrified of what will happen if we set it down.

But confidence in the Architect allows us to rest. It allows us to recognize that we are not the ones holding the universe together, that our existence does not depend on our constant effort, that we are held by a love that does not waver when we are weak or tired or confused.

This does not mean we become passive or irresponsible. We still have our part to play, our lessons to learn, our growth to pursue. But we can engage in this work from a place of rest rather than anxiety, from trust rather than fear.

We can do our best and then let go of the outcome, trusting that the Architect is working in ways we cannot see. We can acknowledge our limitations without being crushed by them, recognizing that we are finite beings and that this is okay.

We can sleep at night, knowing that the universe does not depend on our wakefulness. We can take sabbath, knowing that our worth is not determined by our productivity. We can be still, knowing that we are held in the eternal presence that never sleeps, never wavers, never forgets.

THE JOURNEY CONTINUES

Living in confidence does not mean we have arrived at the destination. We are still in the classroom, still learning, still growing. We still see through a glass, darkly. We still struggle with doubt, with fear, with the gap between what we believe and what we experience.

But confidence gives us the courage to continue the journey. It allows us to face the difficulties ahead—including the profound question of suffering, which we will explore in the next chapter—without being overwhelmed by them. It allows us to hold our beliefs lightly, to remain open to correction and growth, while still committing to a path. It allows us to live with uncertainty while still trusting that we are moving toward a destination of love and knowledge.

The eternal reward is not yet fully realized. We have not yet graduated from the classroom. We have not yet experienced the direct, unmediated knowledge of the Architect that is our ultimate purpose.

But we can live now as though that reward is real, as though we are moving toward it, as though we are held by the love that created us and calls us home. We can live in confidence, trusting that our existence is intentional, our journey is meaningful, and our destination is secure.

This is the invitation: to live as though you are seen, known, loved, and held. To act with courage in the face of uncertainty. To rest in the trust that you are not alone.

The lights are on. The witness is awake. The journey continues.

Pause here. Before moving to the next chapter, sit with this question: What would change in your life if you truly believed you were intentional, that your existence has purpose, that you are moving toward infinite love? This is not a rhetorical question. This is an invitation to transformation.

CHAPTER 6

—

THE ARCHITECTURE
OF SUFFERING

"We also glory in our sufferings,
because we know that suffering
produces perseverance; perseverance,
character; and character, hope."
— Romans 5:3-4

If the universe is designed by a loving Architect, if our existence is intentional and our destination is infinite love, then why is there suffering?

This is perhaps the oldest and most difficult question in theology and philosophy. It is the question that has driven countless people away from faith, the question that seems to contradict everything we have explored so far.

If the Architect is all-powerful and all-loving, why does the classroom include pain? Why are the lessons taught through loss, through illness, through heartbreak, through the thousand natural shocks that flesh is heir to?

This chapter will not provide easy answers, because there are no easy answers. Suffering is real, and it is terrible, and any attempt to explain it away or minimize it is both intellectually dishonest and morally obscene. But we can explore the architecture of suffering—the way pain is woven into the structure of the classroom, the lessons it teaches that cannot be learned any other way, the role it plays in preparing us for the eternal reward.

This exploration requires both intellectual honesty and spiritual sensitivity. We must be willing to sit with the difficulty, to acknowledge the genuine problem, to resist the temptation to offer cheap comfort or simplistic explanations.

6.1 WHY PAIN EXISTS IN A LOVING DESIGN

THE PROBLEM OF EVIL

Let us begin by stating the problem clearly. The existence of suffering seems to contradict the existence of an all-powerful, all-loving Architect. This is sometimes formulated as a logical argument:

If the Architect is all-powerful, the Architect can prevent suffering. If the Architect is all-loving, the Architect wants to prevent suffering. Suffering exists.

Therefore, either the Architect is not all-powerful, or not all-loving, or does not exist. This argument has force, and we must take it seriously. We cannot simply dismiss it or pretend it does not pose a genuine challenge to the framework we have been developing.

But the argument rests on certain assumptions that may not be correct. It assumes that an all-loving being would necessarily prevent all suffering. It assumes that the existence of suffering is incompatible with a good and intentional design.

These assumptions seem obvious—of course a loving parent would prevent their child from suffering if they could. But the relationship between the Architect and creation is not exactly like the relationship between a human parent and child, and the purposes of the classroom may require what seems, from our limited perspective, to be unnecessary pain.

THE NECESSITY OF NATURAL LAW

Let us begin with the most basic form of suffering: physical pain caused by natural processes. You touch a hot stove and burn your hand. You fall and break your bone. You contract an illness and experience fever, nausea, weakness.

Why does the universe operate according to laws that permit these harms? Why didn't the Architect create a reality where fire does not burn, where falls do not injure, where disease does not exist? The answer is that a universe without consistent natural laws would not be a universe at all—it would be chaos. For conscious beings to exist, to learn, to grow, there must be a stable, predictable environment in which actions have consequences.

If fire sometimes burned and sometimes did not, if gravity sometimes worked and sometimes did not, if the same action produced different results each time, we could not learn anything. We could not develop understanding, make plans, or exercise agency. We would be helpless in a world of arbitrary, unpredictable events.

Natural laws create the conditions for learning. They allow us to understand cause and effect, to predict outcomes, to make choices based on our understanding of how the world works. This is essential for the development of consciousness and agency.

But natural laws, by their nature, operate impersonally. Fire burns whatever it touches, whether that is a log or a hand. Gravity pulls on all objects, whether they are safely on the ground or falling from a height. Viruses replicate in whatever host they find, whether that host is ready for the challenge or not.

This impersonality is not a flaw; it is a feature. It is what makes the universe reliable, knowable, navigable. But it also means that natural processes will sometimes cause harm to conscious beings. This is not because the Architect desires our suffering, but because the alternative—a universe without consistent laws—would make consciousness and learning impossible.

THE GIFT OF VULNERABILITY

But there is a deeper reason why suffering exists in a loving design: vulnerability is necessary for certain kinds of growth and relationship.

Consider: if you could not be hurt, what would courage mean? If you could not lose anything, what would sacrifice mean? If you could not suffer, what would compassion mean?

Many of the qualities we most value—bravery, generosity, empathy, perseverance, hope—only make sense in a context where we are vulnerable, where we can be harmed, where we face real risks and real losses.

A being that is invulnerable, that cannot suffer, that has nothing to lose, might be powerful, but it would not be capable of the kind of moral and spiritual growth that the classroom is designed to produce.

Think about the difference between a video game played with invincibility mode turned on versus one where your character can actually die. In the first case, there are no stakes, no tension, no real challenge. You might enjoy the spectacle, but you are not truly engaged. You are not learning, not growing, not being tested.

But when there are real consequences, when you can actually fail, the game becomes meaningful. Your choices matter. Your skills develop. Your victories are earned.

The universe is not a game, and suffering is not entertainment. But the principle holds: for growth to be real, for choices to be meaningful, for character to be developed, there must be genuine vulnerability. We must be able to be hurt, to fail, to lose.

This vulnerability is a gift, even though it does not feel like one. It is what makes our existence significant rather than trivial, what makes our choices matter rather than being mere preferences, what makes our relationships deep rather than superficial.

THE PROBLEM OF DEGREE

But even if we accept that some suffering is necessary for growth, we still face the problem of degree. Why is there so much suffering? Why is it so severe? Why do children die of cancer? Why do natural disasters kill thousands? Why is there torture, genocide, abuse?

Surely the lessons could be taught with less pain. Surely the classroom could be designed with less cruelty. The existence of extreme suffering seems to exceed any pedagogical purpose.

This is the hardest part of the problem, and I will not pretend to have a complete answer. The reality of extreme suffering is a genuine mystery, a place where our understanding fails and we are left with questions that have no satisfying resolution.

But we can make a few observations that may provide some context, even if they do not fully resolve the difficulty.

First, much of the worst suffering is caused not by natural processes but by human choices. War, oppression, abuse, exploitation—these are not features of the Architect's design but consequences of human agency exercised in destructive ways.

The Architect created beings with genuine freedom, genuine otherness, genuine capacity to choose. This freedom is necessary for relationship, for moral growth, for the development of character. But freedom necessarily includes the possibility of choosing wrongly, of causing harm, of inflicting suffering on others.

The Architect could have prevented this by creating beings without freedom, beings who could only choose good. But such beings would be automatons, not persons. They could not enter into genuine relationship, could not grow morally, could not become the kind of beings capable of the eternal reward.

So the Architect accepts the risk of human freedom, knowing that it will sometimes be used destructively. This does not make the Architect responsible for the evil that humans choose, but it does mean that the Architect permits it as a consequence of the greater good of freedom.

Second, our perspective on suffering is necessarily limited. We experience suffering in the moment, in the intensity of pain, in the immediacy of loss. We cannot see the larger pattern, the way our suffering might contribute to growth we cannot yet perceive, the way it might connect to purposes we cannot yet understand.

This is not to say that all suffering has a clear purpose that we would recognize if we could just see the bigger picture. Some suffering may be genuinely pointless, a consequence of living in a universe governed by natural laws and populated by free beings.

But it is to say that our judgment about what is necessary or excessive is made from a very limited vantage point. We see a single frame of the movie and declare it meaningless, not knowing how it fits into the larger story.

THE SOLIDARITY OF THE ARCHITECT

Finally, and most importantly, the Architect does not stand apart from suffering, observing it from a safe distance. In the Christian tradition, which informs much of this book's framework, the Architect enters into the suffering of creation.

God becomes human in Jesus Christ and experiences the full range of human suffering: poverty, rejection, betrayal, torture, death. The Architect does not merely permit suffering; the Architect participates in it, bears it, transforms it from within.

This does not explain why suffering exists, but it does change the nature of the question. The Architect is not a distant designer who creates a painful world and then abandons us to endure it. The Architect is present in the pain, suffering alongside us, holding us in the midst of it.

This solidarity does not make the suffering less real or less terrible. But it does mean that we are not alone in it. The presence that created us and knows us and loves us is also the presence that suffers with us and promises that suffering is not the final word.

6.2 WHAT COMFORT CANNOT TEACH

THE LIMITS OF EASE

If we accept that suffering exists for reasons connected to the nature of the classroom, we must ask: What does suffering teach that comfort cannot?

This is not to romanticize suffering or to suggest that we should seek it out. Suffering is not good in itself; it is terrible, destructive, something to be alleviated whenever possible. But it is to recognize that suffering, when it comes, can teach lessons that are not available through ease and pleasure.

Let us begin with the most obvious: suffering teaches us our limitations. When everything is going well, when we are healthy and successful and surrounded by love, it is easy to believe that we are self-sufficient, that we have everything under control, that we do not need anything beyond ourselves.

But suffering shatters this illusion. When we are sick, we discover that we cannot heal ourselves through willpower. When we are grieving, we discover that we cannot think our way out of pain. When we are facing circumstances beyond our control, we discover that our agency has limits.

This recognition of limitation is humbling, and humility is essential for spiritual growth. As long as we believe we are self-sufficient, we cannot open ourselves to dependence on the Architect. As long as we believe we have everything under control, we cannot surrender to a wisdom greater than our own.

Suffering breaks down the walls of self-sufficiency and creates space for dependence, for trust, for the recognition that we need something beyond ourselves. This is painful, but it is also liberating. It frees us from the exhausting burden of trying to be our own savior.

THE DEVELOPMENT OF COMPASSION

Suffering also teaches compassion in a way that comfort cannot. When we have experienced pain, we develop the capacity to recognize and respond to the pain of others.

Someone who has never suffered may feel sympathy for those who are suffering—an intellectual recognition that their situation is difficult. But sympathy is not the same as compassion. Compassion is the ability to suffer with another, to enter into their experience, to feel their pain as real and significant.

This capacity is developed through our own suffering. When we have been broken, we recognize brokenness in others. When we have been lost, we can sit with others in their lostness without needing to fix them or offer false comfort. When we have been in the darkness, we can be present to others in their darkness without fear. This is one of the most profound gifts that suffering can give: the ability to be truly present to others in their pain. Not to explain it away, not to minimize it, not to rush them through it, but to sit with them, to acknowledge the reality of what they are experiencing, to offer the solidarity of shared suffering.

The world desperately needs people who can do this—people who have been broken and have allowed their brokenness to open them to the brokenness of others. These are the people who can offer genuine comfort, not the cheap comfort of platitudes and easy answers, but the deep comfort of presence and understanding.

THE REFINEMENT OF CHARACTER

Suffering also refines character in ways that ease cannot. When we face difficulty, we discover what we are made of. We learn whether our values are genuine or merely theoretical. We develop strength, perseverance, courage, hope.

Think of the metaphor of refining metal. The ore contains both valuable metal and impurities. To separate them, the ore must be heated to extreme temperatures. The heat does not create the metal—it was always there—but it reveals it, purifies it, makes it useful.

Suffering works similarly in human character. It does not create virtue, but it reveals and refines it. It burns away the superficial, the false, the merely performative, and leaves what is genuine.

This is why people who have suffered deeply often have a quality of authenticity that those who have lived easy lives lack. They have been tested. They have faced themselves in extremity. They have discovered what remains when everything else is stripped away.

This does not mean that suffering automatically produces virtue. People can respond to suffering in destructive ways—becoming bitter, closed, cruel. The refining fire can harden as well as purify.

But when suffering is met with openness, with honesty, with the willingness to learn, it can produce a depth of character that is not available through any other means. It can develop in us the qualities we will need for the eternal reward: authenticity, humility, compassion, strength, hope.

THE DEEPENING OF FAITH

Perhaps most importantly, suffering deepens faith in a way that comfort cannot. Easy faith—the faith that emerges when everything is going well—is often shallow, untested, more like optimism than genuine trust.

But faith that survives suffering, that persists through darkness, that continues to trust even when there is no evidence that trust is warranted—this is faith that has been tested and proven genuine.

The biblical tradition is full of this kind of faith. Job, who loses everything and still refuses to curse God. Abraham, who is willing to sacrifice his son in trust that God's purposes are good. Jesus, who prays in the garden, "Not my will, but yours," even as he faces torture and death.

This is not blind faith that ignores reality or refuses to acknowledge difficulty. It is faith that looks directly at the darkness and still chooses to trust. It is faith that says, "I do not understand, but I will not let go. I cannot see the purpose, but I will continue to believe there is one. I am in pain, but I am not abandoned."

This kind of faith cannot be taught through words or arguments. It can only be developed through experience, through the actual practice of trusting when trust is difficult, of hoping when hope seems foolish, of loving when love is costly.

Suffering provides the conditions for this development. It creates the crucible in which shallow faith is either burned away or transformed into something deeper, stronger, more real.

THE PREPARATION FOR JOY

Finally, suffering prepares us for joy in a way that constant pleasure cannot. This may seem paradoxical, but it is a truth that many who have suffered deeply can attest to.

When you have been in darkness, you appreciate light in a way that someone who has never experienced darkness cannot. When you have been hungry, you savor food with a gratitude that someone who has always been fed cannot match. When you have been lost, you experience the joy of being found with an intensity that someone who has never been lost cannot imagine.

Suffering creates capacity for joy. It deepens our appreciation, sharpens our awareness, makes us grateful for what we might otherwise take for granted. It teaches us that joy is not the absence of suffering but the presence of meaning, connection, love in the midst of a world that includes suffering.

This is not to say that we should seek suffering in order to appreciate joy. That would be perverse. But it is to recognize that when suffering comes—and it will come, because we live in a world governed by natural laws and populated by free beings—it can deepen our capacity for the joy that is our ultimate destination.

The eternal reward is not merely the absence of suffering. It is the presence of infinite love, perfect knowledge, complete communion with the Architect. And our capacity to receive this reward, to experience it fully, to respond to it appropriately, is developed in part through our experience of suffering in the classroom.

6.3 SUFFERING AS SACRED CURRICULUM

THE PEDAGOGY OF PAIN

We have explored why suffering exists and what it can teach. Now we must ask: How do we engage with suffering in a way that allows it to fulfill its pedagogical purpose? How do we suffer well?

This is a delicate question, because it can easily slide into victim-blaming or the suggestion that people who are suffering are somehow failing if they do not respond in the "right" way. We must be very clear: there is no obligation to find meaning in suffering, no requirement to be grateful for pain, no expectation that you should respond to tragedy with spiritual maturity.

Suffering is terrible, and sometimes the only appropriate response is to cry out in anguish, to protest the injustice, to rage against the darkness. The biblical tradition includes this kind of response—the Psalms are full of lament, of complaint, of desperate pleas for relief.

But having said that, we can still observe that some ways of engaging with suffering are more conducive to growth than others. Some responses open us to the lessons suffering can teach, while others close us off and leave us merely damaged rather than refined.

THE PRACTICE OF LAMENT

The first practice is lament—the honest expression of pain, grief, anger, and confusion. Lament is not the same as despair. Despair says, "There is no meaning, no hope, no purpose." Lament says, "This is terrible, and I do not understand it, but I am still here, still speaking, still in relationship."

The Psalms of lament follow a pattern: they begin with honest expression of suffering, they move through complaint and questioning, and they often (though not always) end with a statement of trust or hope. This pattern models a healthy engagement with suffering.

We do not need to pretend that everything is fine. We do not need to suppress our pain or put on a brave face. We can cry out, we can question, we can express our anger and confusion. This honesty is not a failure of faith; it is an expression of faith, because it assumes that there is someone listening, someone who cares, someone to whom our suffering matters.

Lament keeps us in relationship even when we do not understand. It allows us to be authentic about our pain while still maintaining connection with the Architect. It creates space for both suffering and trust to coexist.

THE PRACTICE OF PRESENCE

The second practice is presence—the willingness to be fully present to our suffering rather than trying to escape it or numb it or rush through it.

Our culture encourages us to avoid pain at all costs. We are offered endless distractions, medications, entertainments to keep us from feeling what we are feeling. And while there is a place for pain relief and healthy distraction, there is also a danger in never allowing ourselves to fully experience our suffering.

When we are present to our pain, we can learn from it. We can notice what it reveals about our attachments, our fears, our deepest values. We can allow it to break down our defenses and open us to truth we might otherwise avoid.

This does not mean wallowing in suffering or refusing help. It means being willing to sit with the pain, to feel it fully, to let it do its work in us. It means resisting the temptation to immediately explain it away or find the silver lining or move on to the next thing.

Presence to suffering is difficult, and it often requires support—the presence of others who can sit with us in our pain, who can bear witness to our experience, who can remind us that we are not alone. This is one of the most important gifts we can offer each other: the willingness to be present to another's suffering without trying to fix it or minimize it.

THE PRACTICE OF SURRENDER

The third practice is surrender—the willingness to let go of our demand that reality be other than it is, to accept what we cannot change, to trust that we are held even in the midst of suffering.

Surrender is not the same as resignation. Resignation says, "Nothing matters, so I give up." Surrender says, "I cannot control this, but I can trust that I am not alone in it."

Surrender does not mean we stop working to alleviate suffering—our own or others'. We still seek healing, still pursue justice, still work to make the world less painful. But we do so from a place of acceptance rather than desperate grasping, from trust rather than fear.

This is perhaps the hardest practice, because it requires us to let go of our illusion of control. We want to believe that if we just try hard enough, think clearly enough, do everything right, we can prevent suffering. But we cannot. We are finite beings in a world governed by natural laws and populated by free agents. Suffering will come, regardless of our efforts to prevent it.

Surrender is the recognition of this reality and the choice to trust anyway. It is the prayer of Jesus in the garden: "Not my will, but yours." It is the acknowledgment that we do not understand the full picture, that we cannot see the purposes at work, but that we will continue to trust in the goodness of the Architect.

THE PRACTICE OF MEANING-MAKING

The fourth practice is meaning-making—the active work of finding or creating meaning in our suffering, of integrating it into our larger story, of allowing it to contribute to our growth rather than merely diminishing us.

This is not the same as saying that suffering happens for a reason or that everything works out for the best. Some suffering may be genuinely pointless, a consequence of living in a world that includes randomness and freedom. We do not need to pretend otherwise.

But even when suffering has no inherent meaning, we can choose to give it meaning. We can decide how we will respond to it, what we will learn from it, how we will allow it to shape us. We can take what is terrible and transform it into something that contributes to our growth, our compassion, our depth.

Viktor Frankl, who survived the Nazi concentration camps, wrote about this capacity in "Man's Search for Meaning." He observed that even in the most extreme suffering, people retained the freedom to choose their attitude, to find meaning in their experience, to decide who they would become in response to what they endured.

This is not easy, and it is not always possible in the midst of acute suffering. Sometimes we can only survive, only endure, only get through the next moment. But over time, as we gain distance from the immediate pain, we can engage in the work of meaning-making, of integrating our suffering into our larger story.

THE PRACTICE OF SOLIDARITY

The fifth practice is solidarity—the recognition that we do not suffer alone, that our pain connects us to the suffering of others, that we are part of a larger community of broken beings learning to trust in the midst of darkness.

When we are suffering, it is easy to feel isolated, to believe that no one else understands, that we are uniquely cursed or abandoned. But the truth is that suffering is universal. Every human being experiences pain, loss, grief, fear. We are all in the classroom together, all learning the same difficult lessons.

This recognition can be comforting. It reminds us that we are not alone, that others have walked this path before us, that there is wisdom and support available from those who have suffered and survived. But it also calls us to responsibility. When we have suffered, we have a particular capacity to offer comfort and understanding to others who are suffering. We can be present to them in ways that those who have not suffered cannot. We can offer the solidarity of shared experience, the assurance that they are not alone, the hope that comes from seeing someone who has endured and emerged.

This is one of the ways that suffering can be redemptive—not because the suffering itself is good, but because it can be transformed into compassion, into service, into the capacity to ease the suffering of others.

THE MYSTERY REMAINS

Even after all this exploration, the problem of suffering remains a mystery. We have not solved it or explained it away. We have not made it less terrible or less real.

What we have done is to explore the architecture of suffering—the way it is woven into the structure of the classroom, the lessons it can teach, the practices that can help us engage with it in ways that contribute to growth rather than merely damage.

But we must be humble about our understanding. We see through a glass, darkly. We do not know why some people suffer more than others, why some suffering seems to serve no purpose, why the classroom includes so much pain.

What we can trust is that the Architect is present in the suffering, that we are not alone in it, that it is not the final word. The classroom is temporary. The suffering will end. And what remains is the relationship for which we were created, the love that holds us even in the darkest moments, the joy that will make all the pain seem, in retrospect, like a brief and necessary passage.

This is not an answer that satisfies the intellect. But it may be an answer that sustains the heart, that allows us to continue trusting even when we do not understand, that gives us the courage to remain open to the lessons suffering can teach.

Pause here. Before moving to the next chapter, sit with your own experience of suffering. What has it taught you? How has it shaped you? Where have you found meaning, and where does the mystery remain?

This is sacred ground. Walk carefully.

PART III

THE PRACTICE OF AWAKENING

CHAPTER 7

THE ILLUSION OF SEPARATION

> "The eye cannot say to the hand,
> 'I don't need you!'
> And the head cannot say to the feet,
> 'I don't need you!'"
>
> — 1 Corinthians 12:21

We have explored consciousness as the witness that actualizes reality, the Block Universe as the predetermined structure of spacetime, the impossibility of hiding from the Architect, and the role of suffering in the classroom. Now we must examine one of the deepest illusions that shapes human experience: the illusion of separation.

We experience ourselves as isolated individuals, separate from other beings, separate from the world, separate from the Architect. We feel ourselves to be discrete units of consciousness, bounded by our skin, contained within our skulls, fundamentally alone.

But this experience of separation, while real and powerful, is not the deepest truth about our existence. At a more fundamental level, we are interconnected, interdependent, woven into a web of relationships that constitutes the very fabric of reality.

This chapter will explore the illusion of separation and the reality of connection. We will examine how the witness is not truly isolated, how consciousness connects all things, and how recognizing our interconnection transforms our understanding of ourselves and our relationship with the Architect.

7.1 THE MYTH OF THE ISOLATED SELF

THE EXPERIENCE OF INDIVIDUALITY

Let us begin by acknowledging the reality of individual experience. You are reading these words right now, and your experience of reading them is yours alone. No one else has access to your inner life, your thoughts, your feelings, your sensations.

This privacy of consciousness is fundamental to what it means to be a person. You have a perspective that is uniquely yours, a vantage point from which you witness reality that no one else can occupy. Your experiences are immediate to you in a way they can never be to anyone else.

This individuality is not an illusion. It is real, and it is important. It is what makes you a distinct person rather than merely a part of some larger collective consciousness. It is what makes relationship possible—you can only relate to another if you are genuinely other than them.

But the problem arises when we mistake this real individuality for complete separation. When we assume that because our experience is private, we are therefore isolated. When we believe that the boundaries of our skin mark the boundaries of our being.

This is the myth of the isolated self: the belief that we are fundamentally separate, that we exist independently of everything else, that we are self-contained units navigating a world of other self-contained units.

THE CULTURAL REINFORCEMENT OF SEPARATION

This myth is deeply embedded in modern Western culture. We celebrate individualism, self-reliance, independence. We are taught to think of ourselves as autonomous agents, responsible for our own success or failure, defined by our individual achievements and possessions.

Our economic systems reinforce this myth. We compete for scarce resources, we accumulate private property, we measure our worth by our individual productivity and consumption. The market treats us as isolated units of self-interest, maximizing our own utility without regard for the larger whole.

Our political systems reinforce it as well. We think of rights as belonging to individuals, of freedom as the absence of interference from others, of society as a collection of separate persons who have agreed to certain rules for mutual benefit.

Even our language reinforces the myth. We speak of "my" thoughts, "my" feelings, "my" body, as though these things are possessions that belong to a separate self. We use pronouns that emphasize distinction—I and you, us and them—that create linguistic boundaries between beings. None of this is entirely wrong. Individual rights matter. Personal responsibility matters. The distinction between self and other matters. But when these truths are absolutized, when they become the whole story rather than part of the story, they create a distorted picture of reality.

They make us forget that we are not actually self-sufficient, that we depend on countless others for our existence, that we are embedded in systems and relationships that constitute who we are.

THE ILLUSION EXAMINED

Let us examine the myth more carefully. What does it mean to say that you are a separate, independent self?

Consider your body. It seems like a clear boundary—your skin marks where you end and the world begins. But is this really true?

Your body is constantly exchanging matter and energy with the environment. You breathe in air and breathe out air. You consume food and water and excrete waste. The atoms that make up your body are not permanent; they are constantly being replaced. The "you" of seven years ago shares almost no atoms with the "you" of today.

So where is the boundary? At what point does the air stop being "not you" and become "you"? When does the food stop being "not you" and become "you"? The boundary is not as clear as it seems.

Consider your mind. Your thoughts seem private, contained within your skull. But where do your thoughts come from?

You think in a language you did not invent. You use concepts you learned from others. Your beliefs are shaped by your culture, your education, your relationships. Your very capacity for thought depends on a brain that was formed through interaction with caregivers, that developed in response to environmental stimuli, that continues to be shaped by your experiences.

Even your sense of self—your feeling of being a distinct "I"—is not something you were born with. It developed over time, through interaction with others, through the internalization of how others see you and respond to you.

So where is the boundary between your mind and the minds of others? Between your thoughts and the cultural matrix that shapes them? Again, the boundary is not as clear as it seems.

THE RELATIONAL SELF

What emerges from this examination is a different picture of the self: not as an isolated, independent entity, but as a nexus of relationships, a pattern of interactions, a process rather than a thing.

You are not separate from the world; you are a particular way that the world is organized, a particular pattern of matter and energy and information that has achieved self-awareness.

You are not separate from other beings; you are constituted by your relationships with them, shaped by your interactions, defined in part by how you are seen and known and loved.

You are not separate from the Architect; you exist within the consciousness that grounds all reality, you are held in the eternal gaze that sees all moments simultaneously, you are a thought in the mind of God.

This does not mean you are not real or that your individuality is an illusion. You are real, and you are distinct. But your reality and your distinctness exist within a larger web of connection and interdependence.

Think of a wave in the ocean. The wave is real—you can see it, measure it, distinguish it from other waves. But the wave is not separate from the ocean. It is a particular pattern of movement in the water, a temporary form that the ocean takes. The wave exists because of the ocean, within the ocean, as an expression of the ocean. Similarly, you are a real and distinct pattern of consciousness, but you exist because of the larger reality that grounds you, within that reality, as an expression of that reality. You are a wave in the ocean of being, a thought in the mind of the Architect, a witness through whom the universe becomes aware of itself.

THE IMPLICATIONS OF CONNECTION

Recognizing that we are not truly separate has profound implications for how we understand ourselves and how we live.

If we are not isolated individuals but interconnected beings, then what happens to others affects us. Their suffering is our suffering. Their flourishing is our flourishing. We cannot be fully well while others are sick, cannot be fully free while others are oppressed, cannot be fully at peace while others are in turmoil.

This is not just a moral claim—though it is that—but a metaphysical one. At the deepest level, we are not separate. The boundaries between us are real but permeable, important but not absolute. We are members of one another, parts of a larger whole, waves in the same ocean.

This recognition calls us to compassion, to solidarity, to the recognition that the other is not truly other but is, in some deep sense, another expression of the same reality that expresses itself in us.

It also calls us to humility. If we are not self-sufficient, if we depend on countless others for our existence and our flourishing, then we cannot take credit for our achievements as though they were ours alone. We are who we are because of the web of relationships that sustains us, the community that shapes us, the Architect who grounds us.

And it calls us to gratitude. Every moment of our existence is a gift, not just from the Architect but from the countless beings whose lives and actions make our lives possible. We are recipients of an inheritance we did not earn, beneficiaries of a generosity we can never fully repay.

7.2 HOW WITNESSING CONNECTS ALL THINGS

THE SHARED ACT OF CONSCIOUSNESS

We have explored consciousness as the witness that actualizes reality, the presence that turns potential into actual by observing and naming. But we have mostly discussed this as an individual act—you, the witness, encountering the world.

Now we must expand this understanding. Witnessing is not just an individual act; it is a shared act, a collective participation in the ongoing creation of reality. When you witness the blue ball in the darkness, you are not creating its blueness out of nothing. The ball has properties that exist independently of your observation—wavelengths of light it reflects, molecular structures that determine those wavelengths. Your witnessing actualizes these properties, brings them into the realm of experienced reality, but it does not create them arbitrarily.

And crucially, other witnesses can observe the same ball and agree that it is blue. Your witnessing and their witnessing converge on the same reality. This convergence is what makes objective knowledge possible, what allows us to build shared understanding, what creates the common world we inhabit together.

This shared witnessing is a form of connection. When we observe the same reality, when our experiences converge, when we can communicate about what we have witnessed and find agreement, we are participating in something larger than our individual consciousness.

We are co-creating the world, not in the sense that we are making it up, but in the sense that we are collectively actualizing it, bringing it into the realm of shared experience, making it real in a way that transcends any individual perspective.

THE INTERSUBJECTIVITY OF MEANING

This becomes even clearer when we consider meaning rather than just physical properties. The ball is blue—that is a fact about wavelengths and perception. But what does blueness mean? What associations does it carry? What emotions does it evoke?

These meanings are not purely individual. They are shaped by culture, by shared symbols, by collective experience. Blue might mean sadness in one context, tranquility in another, royalty in another. These meanings are created and sustained through shared understanding, through the convergence of many witnesses who agree on what blue signifies.

Language itself is the most obvious example of this intersubjectivity. Words have meaning only because we agree on what they mean. The sound "blue" refers to a particular color only because English speakers have collectively decided that it does. The meaning exists in the space between us, in the shared understanding that makes communication possible.

But this extends far beyond language. All of culture—art, music, ritual, custom, law—exists in this intersubjective space. It is real, but its reality depends on shared witnessing, on collective participation, on the convergence of many consciousnesses creating and sustaining meaning together. This means that we are connected through our participation in shared meaning-making. When you understand what I mean by "blue," when you grasp the significance of a symbol, when you participate in a cultural practice, you are entering into a shared consciousness, a collective witnessing that transcends individual minds.

THE WITNESS AND THE WITNESSED

But there is an even deeper connection revealed through witnessing. When you witness another person, you are not just observing an object. You are encountering another witness, another consciousness, another center of experience.

This creates a unique kind of relationship. The other person is both witnessed (an object of your observation) and witness (a subject with their own perspective). They see you even as you see them. They witness you witnessing them.

This mutual witnessing creates a feedback loop, a relationship that is more than the sum of its parts. You are shaped by how they see you. They are shaped by how you see them. Your witnessing affects their self-understanding, and their witnessing affects yours.

Think about how you become aware of yourself through the eyes of others. A child develops self-consciousness by internalizing how their caregivers see them. An adult's sense of identity is shaped by how they are recognized and responded to by others.

We do not know ourselves directly; we know ourselves through the mirror of other witnesses. We see ourselves reflected in their eyes, their words, their responses. Our very sense of being a self is constituted through this mutual witnessing.

This means that we are not just connected to others through shared observation of the world. We are connected through the way we witness each other, the way we participate in each other's self-understanding, the way we co-create each other's identity through our mutual recognition.

THE ARCHITECT AS ULTIMATE WITNESS

And all of this witnessing—individual and collective, of the world and of each other—takes place within the witnessing of the Architect.

We have discussed the Architect's omniscience, the fact that nothing is hidden from the divine gaze. But now we can see this in a new light: the Architect is the ultimate witness, the consciousness within which all other witnessing takes place.

When you witness the blue ball, you are participating in the Architect's witnessing of creation. When you witness another person, you are participating in the Architect's witnessing of that person. When you witness yourself, you are participating in the Architect's witnessing of you.

Your consciousness is not separate from the Architect's consciousness; it is a particular expression of it, a localized instance of the universal witnessing that grounds all reality.

This is a profound mystery, and we must be careful not to collapse the distinction between creature and Creator. You are not identical with the Architect. You have your own perspective, your own experience, your own agency. The Architect is infinitely greater than you, transcendent as well as immanent.

But neither are you completely separate from the Architect. You exist within the divine consciousness, you participate in the divine witnessing, you are a thought in the mind of God that has achieved its own capacity for thought.

This means that when you witness anything—the world, another person, yourself—you are participating in the Architect's ongoing relationship with creation. You are a means by which the Architect knows the world, loves the world, brings the world into fuller reality.

THE ETHICAL IMPLICATIONS

This understanding of witnessing as connection has profound ethical implications. If we are connected through our mutual witnessing, if we participate in each other's self-understanding, if we are all expressions of the Architect's consciousness, then how we witness matters enormously.

When you witness another person with love, with respect, with genuine attention, you are participating in the Architect's loving gaze. You are helping to actualize their full humanity, to call forth their deepest potential, to affirm their sacred worth.

But when you witness another person with contempt, with objectification, with indifference, you are distorting the Architect's witnessing. You are reducing them to less than they are, denying their full humanity, participating in their diminishment rather than their flourishing.

This is why the great ethical traditions emphasize the importance of how we see others. "Love your neighbor as yourself" is not just a moral command; it is a recognition of the deep truth that your neighbor is, in some sense, yourself—another expression of the same reality, another wave in the same ocean, another witness participating in the same act of consciousness.

When you harm another, you harm yourself. When you diminish another, you diminish yourself. When you fail to see another truly, you fail to see yourself truly. Because at the deepest level, you are not separate.

7.3 THE WEB OF CONSCIOUSNESS

THE METAPHOR OF INDRA'S NET

There is an ancient Buddhist metaphor that captures the interconnection of all things: Indra's Net. Imagine an infinite net stretching in all directions. At each node of the net is a jewel, and each jewel reflects all the other jewels in the net.

This means that if you look closely at any single jewel, you can see the entire net reflected in it. And if you change one jewel, the reflection in all the other jewels changes as well. Each part contains the whole, and each part affects all the other parts.

This is a powerful image for understanding the web of consciousness. Each individual consciousness is like a jewel in the net—distinct, real, particular. But each consciousness also reflects all the others, contains the whole in some sense, and is affected by changes in any other part.

You are not just connected to other beings; you are constituted by your connections. Your consciousness is what it is because of its relationships, its position in the web, its reflections of and responses to all the other nodes of awareness.

THE SCIENTIFIC PICTURE

This metaphor finds surprising support in modern science. Physics tells us that at the quantum level, particles that have interacted remain connected in a phenomenon called entanglement. Change the state of one particle, and the state of its entangled partner changes instantaneously, regardless of the distance between them.

This suggests that at the most fundamental level of reality, separation is not absolute. Things that have been in relationship remain in relationship, connected in ways that transcend space and time.

Biology tells us that all life on Earth is related, descended from common ancestors, sharing genetic material, participating in interconnected ecosystems. You are not separate from the tree outside your window; you share ancestors with it, you depend on it for oxygen, you are part of the same web of life.

Neuroscience tells us that consciousness itself may not be as localized as we think. The boundaries between self and other, between inner and outer, are constructed by the brain and can be altered. People who have experienced ego dissolution through meditation or psychedelics report a sense of unity with all things, a dissolution of the boundaries that normally define the self. None of this proves that we are all one consciousness or that individual identity is an illusion. But it does suggest that the boundaries we experience are not as absolute as they seem, that connection is more fundamental than separation, that we are participants in a larger whole.

THE THEOLOGICAL PICTURE

The theological tradition offers its own vision of interconnection. In Christianity, the doctrine of the Body of Christ teaches that all believers are members of one body, with Christ as the head. Each member has a distinct function, but all are part of the same organism, sharing the same life.

This is not just a metaphor for social organization. It is a claim about ontology, about the nature of reality. When you are united with Christ, you are united with all others who are united with Christ. You participate in a shared life that transcends individual existence.

The doctrine of the Trinity offers an even more profound vision of interconnection. God is not a solitary individual but a communion of persons—Father, Son, and Holy Spirit—who are distinct yet united, three yet one. The very nature of ultimate reality is relational, not isolated.

And if we are created in the image of God, if we are meant to reflect the divine nature, then we too are fundamentally relational. We are not meant to be isolated individuals but persons-in-communion, finding our identity and our fulfillment in relationship rather than in separation.

THE MYSTICAL EXPERIENCE

Throughout history, mystics from various traditions have reported experiences of unity, of the dissolution of boundaries, of direct awareness of the interconnection of all things.

They describe moments when the sense of being a separate self falls away, when they experience themselves as part of a larger whole, when the distinction between self and other, between creature and Creator, becomes permeable or disappears entirely.

These experiences are often described as the most real, most true, most significant moments of their lives. They are not hallucinations or delusions but glimpses of a deeper reality that is normally hidden by the filters of ordinary consciousness.

The mystics tell us that separation is the illusion and connection is the truth. That we are always already united with all things and with the Architect, but we have forgotten this truth, covered it over with layers of ego and fear and the habits of dualistic thinking. The spiritual path, in this view, is not about achieving something new but about remembering what has always been true, removing the obstacles that prevent us from seeing our fundamental interconnection, awakening to the reality that we are not and have never been separate.

LIVING FROM CONNECTION

What does it mean to live from this understanding of connection rather than from the illusion of separation?

It means recognizing that your well-being is inseparable from the well-being of others. That you cannot be fully healthy while others are sick, cannot be fully free while others are oppressed, cannot be fully at peace while others are suffering.

It means approaching others not as strangers or competitors but as kin, as fellow expressions of the same reality, as other jewels in the same net. It means seeing the face of the Architect in every face you encounter.

It means taking responsibility not just for your individual actions but for your participation in systems and structures that affect others. It means recognizing that you are implicated in the suffering caused by your society, your economy, your culture, even when you did not directly cause it. It means practicing compassion, not as a moral obligation imposed from outside but as a natural response to the recognition that the other's suffering is your suffering, that their joy is your joy, that their liberation is inseparable from your own.

This is not easy. The habits of separation run deep. We have been trained since childhood to see ourselves as isolated units competing for scarce resources. We have been taught to protect our interests, to build walls, to distinguish sharply between "us" and "them."

But these habits are based on a misunderstanding of reality. They are strategies developed within the illusion of separation, and they perpetuate that illusion. When we act from separation, we create more separation. When we act from connection, we reveal and strengthen the connection that was always there.

Living from connection means making choices that honor the web of relationships in which you exist. It means asking not just "What do I want?" but "What serves the whole?" It means recognizing that your individual flourishing is bound up with the flourishing of your community, your society, your species, your planet.

It means practicing generosity, knowing that what you give away returns to you through the web of connection. It means practicing forgiveness, knowing that holding resentment poisons the entire system of which you are a part. It means practicing gratitude, knowing that everything you have is a gift from the web of relationships that sustains you.

It means being willing to sacrifice your narrow self-interest for the good of the whole, not out of self-denial but out of the recognition that the whole includes you, that serving the whole is serving your truest self.

This is what the great spiritual traditions have always taught. Love your neighbor as yourself—not because it is a nice thing to do, but because your neighbor is yourself, another expression of the same reality. What you do to the least of these, you do to me—not as metaphor, but as literal truth about the nature of interconnection.

Living from connection transforms everything. It transforms how you eat, recognizing your connection to the soil, the water, the farmers, the countless beings whose lives sustain yours. It transforms how you work, recognizing your participation in systems of production and exchange that affect countless others. It transforms how you consume, recognizing that every purchase is a vote for the kind of world you want to create. It transforms your relationships, moving from transactions to genuine encounter, from using others to meet your needs to recognizing others as sacred expressions of the same reality that expresses itself as you. It transforms your politics, moving from the question "What's in it for me?" to "What serves the common good?"

It transforms your spirituality, moving from the project of individual salvation to the recognition that we are saved together or not at all, that enlightenment is not an individual achievement but a collective awakening to our fundamental interconnection.

This does not mean losing your individuality. Remember: you are a real and distinct pattern in the web, a unique jewel reflecting the light in a way no other jewel can. Your particular gifts, your particular perspective, your particular calling—these matter. The web needs your unique contribution.

But it means holding your individuality lightly, recognizing it as one expression of a larger whole, valuable precisely because of its relationship to the whole. It means being willing to let go of the small self—the ego, the separate identity, the defended boundary—in order to discover the larger Self that includes all beings. This is the great paradox: you must lose your life to find it. You must die to the illusion of separation to be born into the reality of connection. You must surrender the isolated self to discover the Self that is one with all things.

And this surrender is not a loss but a homecoming. It is the return to what you have always been, the remembering of what you have always known, the awakening to the reality that has always been true.

You are not separate. You have never been separate. The isolation you feel is an illusion, a temporary forgetting, a necessary part of the curriculum but not the final truth.

The final truth is connection. The final truth is love. The final truth is that you are a beloved expression of the infinite consciousness that grounds all reality, inseparable from all other expressions, held in a web of relationships that extends through all space and all time.

This is what the Architect has been trying to teach you all along. This is what every moment of your life has been pointing toward. This is the truth that will set you free.

Pause here. Before moving to the next chapter, sit with this recognition of interconnection. How does it feel in your body? What resistance arises? What longing?

The illusion of separation is dissolving. The truth of connection is emerging. Are you ready to live from this truth?

THE PRACTICE OF PRESENCE

"Be still,
and know that I am God."
— Psalm 46:10

We have explored the nature of reality, the structure of time, the impossibility of hiding, the purpose of the universe, the architecture of suffering, and the illusion of separation. We have built a comprehensive framework for understanding consciousness, reality, and divine purpose.

But understanding is not enough. Knowledge that remains merely intellectual, that does not transform how we live, is incomplete. The question now is: How do we embody these truths? How do we move from knowing about reality to participating consciously in it?

The answer is presence.

Presence is the gateway through which all the concepts we have explored become lived experience. It is the practice that dissolves the gap between theory and reality, between knowing and being. It is the discipline that aligns us with the Architect's witnessing and awakens us to our role as conscious participants in the unfolding of reality. This chapter is about how to cultivate presence, why it matters, and what it reveals.

8.1 BECOMING A CONSCIOUS PARTICIPANT

THE DEFAULT MODE: UNCONSCIOUS LIVING

Most of us spend most of our time in a state of semi-consciousness, moving through life on autopilot, lost in thought, disconnected from the present moment.

We eat without tasting, walk without feeling our feet on the ground, talk without really listening, look without really seeing. We are physically present but mentally absent, our attention scattered across past regrets and future anxieties, our awareness fragmented by the constant stream of thoughts, judgments, and narratives running through our minds.

This is what we might call unconscious living—going through the motions of life without being fully present to the experience of living. It is a kind of sleepwalking, a trance state in which we are only dimly aware of the reality unfolding around us and within us.

Why do we live this way? Partly because we have been conditioned to it. Our culture values productivity over presence, doing over being, achievement over awareness. We are taught to focus on goals and outcomes, to plan for the future, to analyze the past, to constantly think about what comes next rather than being fully present to what is happening now.

Partly because presence can be uncomfortable. When we are truly present, we feel everything—not just the pleasant sensations but also the painful ones, not just the joy but also the grief, not just the peace but also the anxiety. It is easier to stay distracted, to keep ourselves busy, to avoid the intensity of direct experience.

And partly because we do not realize there is an alternative. We assume that the semi-conscious state is normal, that the constant mental chatter is just how minds work, that being lost in thought is an inevitable part of being human.

But it is not inevitable. It is a habit, and like all habits, it can be changed.

THE ALTERNATIVE: CONSCIOUS PARTICIPATION

Conscious participation means being fully present to the reality of this moment, awake to the experience of being alive, aware of the witnessing that is happening through you.

It means bringing your full attention to whatever you are doing—eating, walking, working, conversing—so that you are not just going through the motions but genuinely experiencing the activity. It means noticing the sensations in your body, the thoughts in your mind, the emotions in your heart, without getting lost in them, without identifying with them, simply observing them as they arise and pass away.

It means recognizing that you are not just a passive observer of reality but an active participant in it, that your witnessing is part of what makes reality real, that your consciousness is contributing to the actualization of the present moment.

Remember the blue ball in the darkness from Chapter 1. The ball has no color until consciousness names it. Similarly, the present moment has no full reality until consciousness witnesses it. Your presence is not incidental to reality; it is constitutive of it.

When you are fully present, you are fulfilling your role as a witness. You are doing what the Architect invited you to do: turning on the lights, naming what is there, participating in the ongoing creation of reality.

This is not a metaphor. This is the literal truth about the relationship between consciousness and reality. Your presence matters. Your attention matters. Your witnessing matters.

THE PRACTICE OF WAKING UP

How do we move from unconscious living to conscious participation? How do we wake up from the trance of distraction and become present to reality?

The answer is practice. Presence is a skill, and like all skills, it must be developed through repeated effort. We must train ourselves to notice when we have drifted into unconsciousness and gently bring ourselves back to presence.

This is what meditation is: the systematic practice of returning attention to the present moment. You sit quietly, you focus on your breath or a mantra or the sensations in your body, and when your mind wanders (which it will, constantly), you notice that it has wandered and you bring it back.

You do this over and over, thousands of times, and gradually you develop the capacity to remain present for longer periods. You strengthen the muscle of attention. You become more skilled at noticing when you have drifted and more adept at returning.

But meditation is not the only practice. Any activity can become a practice of presence if you bring full attention to it. Washing dishes can be a meditation if you are fully present to the sensation of warm water, the texture of the sponge, the movement of your hands. Walking can be a meditation if you are fully present to the feeling of your feet touching the ground, the rhythm of your breath, the sights and sounds around you.

The key is intention. You must decide to be present. You must choose, moment by moment, to bring your attention back to the reality of now rather than drifting into the fantasies of past and future.

This is harder than it sounds. The mind resists presence. It wants to wander, to plan, to worry, to judge, to narrate. It has been trained for decades to do these things, and it will not give up the habit easily.

But with practice, it becomes easier. The periods of presence become longer. The returns from distraction become quicker. The quality of your awareness becomes clearer, more stable, more luminous.

And as you develop this capacity for presence, something remarkable happens: you begin to see reality more clearly. The fog of mental chatter lifts, and you perceive the world with fresh eyes, as though for the first time.

PRESENCE AND THE BLOCK UNIVERSE

How does presence relate to the Block Universe we explored in Chapter 2?

Remember: the Block Universe is the view that all moments—past, present, and future—exist simultaneously, that time is like a finished film with every frame already printed. From the perspective of eternity, your entire life is a completed pattern, a fixed structure in the four-dimensional fabric of spacetime.

But from your perspective, moving through time, the future is unknown and the present is the only moment you can experience. You cannot step outside the film and see it all at once. You can only experience it frame by frame, moment by moment.

Presence is the practice of fully inhabiting the frame you are in. It is the recognition that this moment—this frame, this now—is the only moment you have direct access to. The past is memory, the future is imagination, but the present is real, immediate, alive.

When you are fully present, you are aligned with the reality of your temporal existence. You are not trying to escape into past or future but accepting the gift of now, the only moment in which you can actually live.

And paradoxically, this acceptance of the present moment connects you to the eternal. Because the present moment is the point of contact between time and eternity, between the Block Universe and your lived experience of it.

When you are fully present, you are touching the eternal now, the timeless reality that underlies the flow of time. You are experiencing the frame not just as a fleeting instant but as a complete reality, a jewel in the net of all moments.

This is why mystics across traditions speak of the eternal present, the now that never ends. They are not denying the reality of time but pointing to the deeper reality that time unfolds within, the eternal consciousness that witnesses all moments simultaneously.

Presence is the practice that opens you to this deeper reality. It is the doorway through which you step from time into eternity, from the film into the awareness that watches the film.

PRESENCE AND DIVINE WITNESSING

Presence also aligns you with the Architect's witnessing.

Remember from Chapter 3: the Architect sees everything, knows everything, witnesses all moments and all secrets with perfect clarity. Nothing is hidden from the divine gaze.

When you are present, you are participating in this witnessing. You are seeing reality as it is, without the distortions of judgment, narrative, or projection. You are witnessing the present moment with clarity, just as the Architect witnesses it. This does not mean you see with the same comprehensiveness as the Architect—you are finite, limited, bound by the constraints of your particular perspective. But it means you are seeing truly, seeing what is actually there rather than what you imagine or fear or hope is there.

Presence is a form of honesty. It is the willingness to see reality as it is rather than as you wish it to be. It is the courage to face what is actually happening in this moment rather than escaping into fantasy or distraction.

And this honesty aligns you with the Architect's truth. When you are present, you are seeing with the eyes of truth, witnessing with the consciousness of truth, participating in the divine act of knowing reality as it is.

This is why presence is so transformative. It is not just a technique for reducing stress or improving focus (though it does those things). It is a spiritual practice that aligns you with the fundamental nature of reality, that connects you to the divine consciousness that grounds all existence.

When you are present, you are fulfilling your purpose as a witness. You are doing what you were created to do. You are participating consciously in the Architect's ongoing act of creation.

THE RESISTANCE TO PRESENCE

If presence is so valuable, why is it so difficult? Why do we resist it?

Partly because presence requires us to feel everything, including what is painful. When we are distracted, we can avoid uncomfortable emotions, difficult truths, painful realities. But when we are present, we feel it all.

The grief we have been avoiding. The anxiety we have been suppressing. The loneliness we have been denying. The anger we have been repressing. Presence brings us face to face with the full reality of our experience, and that can be overwhelming.

This is why many people, when they first begin to practice meditation, find it extremely difficult. They sit down to be present, and immediately they are flooded with uncomfortable thoughts and feelings. The mind races, the body fidgets, the emotions surge. It feels like torture rather than peace.

But this is actually a sign that the practice is working. The discomfort is not a problem to be solved but a reality to be witnessed. The thoughts and feelings have always been there; you are just becoming aware of them for the first time.

And as you continue to practice presence, something shifts. You learn that you can feel difficult emotions without being destroyed by them. You learn that thoughts are just thoughts, not facts. You learn that sensations arise and pass away, that nothing lasts forever, that you are larger than any particular experience.

You develop what Buddhists call equanimity—the capacity to remain present and balanced in the face of both pleasant and unpleasant experiences, neither grasping at the pleasant nor pushing away the unpleasant, simply witnessing what is.

This equanimity is not indifference. It is not a cold detachment or a refusal to care. It is a warm, spacious awareness that can hold all experiences with compassion, that can be present to suffering without being overwhelmed by it.

And this equanimity is itself a form of freedom. When you are no longer controlled by the need to avoid discomfort, when you can be present to whatever arises, you are free to respond to reality rather than react to your fears.

Another reason we resist presence is that it threatens the ego, the sense of separate self that we have constructed through years of identification with thoughts, roles, and narratives.

The ego wants to maintain control, to keep the story going, to preserve the illusion of separation. But presence dissolves these constructions. When you are fully present, there is no story, no role, no separate self—there is only the direct experience of reality, the pure witnessing that precedes all interpretation.

This can feel like death to the ego. And in a sense, it is. Presence is a kind of dying, a letting go of the false self in order to discover the true Self.

But this death is also a birth. What dies is the illusion; what is born is the truth. What dies is the separate self; what is born is the recognition of your fundamental interconnection with all things.

This is the great paradox of presence: you must lose yourself to find yourself. You must die to the ego to be born into your true nature. You must surrender control to discover freedom.

8.2 THE DISCIPLINE OF ATTENTION

ATTENTION AS THE CURRENCY OF CONSCIOUSNESS

If presence is the state we are cultivating, attention is the tool we use to cultivate it. Attention is the capacity to direct consciousness toward a particular object, to focus awareness on a specific aspect of experience.

In our contemporary world, attention has become a scarce and valuable resource. We are constantly bombarded with stimuli competing for our attention—advertisements, notifications, news feeds, entertainment, demands from work and family. Our attention is fragmented, scattered, pulled in a thousand directions at once.

This is not accidental. There is an entire industry dedicated to capturing and monetizing your attention. Social media platforms, streaming services, news organizations, advertisers—all of them are competing to grab your attention and hold it as long as possible, because attention is the currency of the digital economy.

But attention is also the currency of consciousness. Where you place your attention determines what becomes real for you, what you experience, what you know. Your attention shapes your reality.

Remember the blue ball in the darkness. The ball becomes blue when consciousness names it, when attention is directed toward it. Similarly, whatever you give your attention to becomes vivid, real, significant in your experience. Whatever you ignore fades into the background, becomes dim, loses reality.

This means that learning to direct your attention is one of the most important skills you can develop. It is the foundation of presence, the key to conscious participation, the practice that allows you to fulfill your role as a witness.

THE WANDERING MIND

The default state of the untrained mind is wandering. Thoughts arise spontaneously, attention jumps from one thing to another, consciousness drifts through memories, fantasies, plans, worries, judgments, without any intentional direction.

This is sometimes called "monkey mind" in Buddhist tradition—the restless, chattering, undisciplined mind that swings from branch to branch, never settling, never still.

Research in neuroscience confirms this. Studies show that the average person's mind wanders about 47% of the time. Nearly half of our waking hours are spent lost in thought, disconnected from the present moment, our attention scattered and unfocused.

And this wandering is not neutral. Studies also show that mind-wandering is strongly correlated with unhappiness. When our minds wander, we tend to ruminate on problems, replay past hurts, worry about future threats. We are less happy when our minds are wandering than when we are focused on what we are doing, even if what we are doing is not particularly pleasant.

This makes sense in light of what we have explored. When the mind wanders, we are disconnected from reality, lost in mental constructions, separated from the direct experience of the present moment. We are not fulfilling our role as witnesses; we are lost in the fog of our own thoughts.

TRAINING ATTENTION

The good news is that attention can be trained. Just as you can strengthen your muscles through physical exercise, you can strengthen your attention through mental exercise.

This is what meditation does. When you sit in meditation and focus on your breath, you are training your attention. When your mind wanders (which it will), you notice that it has wandered and you bring it back to the breath. You do this over and over, and gradually your attention becomes stronger, more stable, more under your control.

This is not easy. The mind resists discipline. It wants to wander, to follow every thought, to chase every distraction. Training attention requires patience, persistence, and self-compassion.

You will fail constantly. Your mind will wander thousands of times in a single meditation session. You will get frustrated, discouraged, convinced that you are terrible at this and should give up.

But the practice is not about achieving perfect focus. The practice is about noticing when you have wandered and returning. Every time you notice and return, you are strengthening your attention. Every time you bring your mind back to the present moment, you are developing the skill of presence.

Think of it like training a puppy. When the puppy wanders off, you do not punish it; you gently call it back. You do this over and over, with patience and kindness, and gradually the puppy learns to stay close.

Similarly, when your mind wanders, you do not berate yourself; you gently bring it back. You do this over and over, with patience and kindness, and gradually your mind learns to stay present.

DIFFERENT OBJECTS OF ATTENTION

There are many different objects you can use to train attention. The breath is the most common—you focus on the sensation of breathing, the rise and fall of the chest or belly, the feeling of air moving through the nostrils.

But you can also focus on bodily sensations more generally—the feeling of your hands resting in your lap, the pressure of your body against the chair, the subtle sensations throughout your body. This is called body scanning or somatic meditation.

You can focus on sounds—the hum of traffic, the chirping of birds, the silence between sounds. You can focus on visual objects—a candle flame, a mandala, the play of light and shadow.

You can focus on a mantra—a word or phrase repeated silently, such as "peace" or "I am" or a traditional sacred phrase from your spiritual tradition.

You can focus on loving-kindness—generating feelings of goodwill toward yourself and others, silently repeating phrases like "May I be happy, may I be healthy, may I be safe, may I live with ease."

The specific object matters less than the practice of focusing. What you are developing is the capacity to direct attention intentionally and sustain it on a chosen object, rather than allowing it to wander randomly.

Different objects may be more suitable for different people or different purposes. Breath is universal and always available. Body sensations help develop embodied awareness. Sounds help develop receptive attention. Mantras help quiet the verbal mind. Loving-kindness helps develop compassion.

Experiment with different objects and find what works for you. But whatever object you choose, the practice is the same: focus on the object, notice when your mind wanders, gently return your attention to the object. Repeat.

ATTENTION IN DAILY LIFE

Meditation is the formal practice of training attention, but the real test is whether you can bring that trained attention into daily life.

Can you be fully present while eating breakfast, tasting each bite, feeling the texture, noticing the flavors? Or are you eating mechanically while scrolling through your phone or planning your day?

Can you be fully present while walking, feeling your feet on the ground, noticing the movement of your body, seeing the world around you? Or are you walking on autopilot, lost in thought, barely aware of your surroundings?

Can you be fully present while talking with someone, really listening to what they are saying, noticing their facial expressions and body language, feeling the connection between you? Or are you half-listening while thinking about what you will say next or checking your phone?

This is where the practice becomes real. This is where presence transforms from a concept into a lived reality.

The challenge is that daily life is full of distractions and demands. It is easy to be present when you are sitting quietly in meditation. It is much harder when you are rushing to a meeting, dealing with a difficult colleague, managing multiple tasks, responding to constant interruptions. But this is precisely why the practice matters. The point is not to be present only in ideal conditions but to bring presence into the messy, complicated, demanding reality of everyday life.

This requires intention. You must decide, moment by moment, to be present. You must choose to bring your full attention to whatever you are doing, even if it is mundane or difficult.

And you must be patient with yourself. You will forget constantly. You will spend hours lost in distraction before you remember to be present. This is normal. This is part of the practice.

The practice is not about being present all the time. The practice is about remembering to be present more often, about shortening the time between forgetting and remembering, about gradually increasing the percentage of your life that you experience consciously rather than sleepwalking through.

ATTENTION AND LOVE

There is a deep connection between attention and love. To give someone your full attention is an act of love. To really see someone, to really listen to them, to be fully present with them—this is how we communicate that they matter, that they are valued, that they are worthy of our time and energy. Conversely, to withhold attention is a form of rejection. When we are physically present but mentally absent, when we are looking at our phone while someone is talking to us, when we are thinking about something else while pretending to listen—this communicates that the person is not important enough to deserve our full attention.

Children know this instinctively. When a child says "Watch me!" they are not just asking you to look in their direction. They are asking for your full attention, your complete presence. They want to be seen, to be witnessed, to know that what they are doing matters to you.

And when we give them that attention—when we put down our phone, turn off the TV, and really watch them—we are giving them love. We are saying, through our attention, "You matter. What you are doing matters. I see you."

This is true in all relationships. Attention is how we love. Presence is how we honor the sacred in another person.

And this connects back to the Architect's witnessing. The Architect gives you complete attention, sees you fully, knows you perfectly. You are never ignored, never overlooked, never dismissed. You are always seen, always known, always held in the divine gaze. When you give someone your full attention, you are participating in this divine witnessing. You are seeing them as the Architect sees them—as a sacred expression of consciousness, worthy of being fully known.

This is why the practice of attention is not just a technique for personal development. It is a spiritual practice, a way of loving, a participation in the divine act of witnessing reality into being.

8.3 LIVING AS THOUGH YOU ARE SEEN

THE GAZE OF THE ARCHITECT

We explored in Chapter 3 the reality that nothing is hidden from the Architect. The divine consciousness sees all, knows all, witnesses every moment and every secret with perfect clarity.

This is not a theoretical claim. This is the fundamental structure of reality. The Architect exists outside the box of spacetime and sees the entire Block Universe at once. Every thought you have ever had, every action you have ever taken, every secret you have ever kept—all of it is perfectly visible to the divine gaze.

You are always seen. You are always known. You are always witnessed. For many people, this is a terrifying thought. It feels like surveillance, like an invasion of privacy, like a violation of autonomy. We want to have secrets, to have parts of ourselves that are hidden, to maintain control over what others know about us.

But what if we shifted our perspective? What if being seen is not a threat but a gift? What if being known is not a violation but a homecoming?

THE GIFT OF BEING SEEN

Think about the experience of being truly seen by another person. Not just looked at, but really seen—your gifts and your wounds, your strengths and your weaknesses, your beauty and your brokenness.

When someone sees you this way and loves you anyway, it is profoundly healing. It dissolves the shame that comes from hiding. It releases the exhaustion of pretending. It allows you to relax into your authentic self, knowing that you are accepted as you are.

This is what the Architect offers: complete seeing, complete knowing, complete acceptance. You do not have to hide. You do not have to pretend. You do not have to maintain the exhausting performance of being someone you are not.

You are seen, and you are loved. Not despite your flaws, but including them. Not because you have earned it, but because you exist. Not conditionally, but absolutely.

This is grace. This is what the universe is teaching you. This is the lesson of the classroom.

And when you truly understand this—when you really grasp that you are always seen and always loved—it transforms how you live.

LIVING FROM AUTHENTICITY

If you are always seen, there is no point in pretending. The performance is futile. The mask is transparent. The Architect sees through it all.

This can be liberating. It means you can stop trying to manage others' perceptions of you. You can stop curating your image, hiding your weaknesses, exaggerating your strengths. You can simply be who you are.

This does not mean you should be reckless or inconsiderate. It does not mean you should say everything you think or do everything you feel like doing. Wisdom still requires discernment, compassion still requires sensitivity to others' needs.

But it means you can be honest. You can acknowledge your limitations. You can admit when you do not know something. You can ask for help when you need it. You can show your vulnerability without shame.

Living from authenticity means aligning your outer life with your inner truth. It means closing the gap between who you pretend to be and who you actually are. It means having integrity—being integrated, whole, the same person in public and in private.

This is harder than it sounds. We have been trained since childhood to perform, to present an acceptable version of ourselves, to hide the parts that might be rejected. Authenticity requires unlearning these habits, dismantling the protective structures we have built, risking the vulnerability of being truly seen.

But it is also deeply freeing. When you stop pretending, you stop exhausting yourself. When you stop hiding, you stop living in fear of being discovered. When you accept that you are already seen, you can relax into the truth of who you are.

LIVING FROM ACCOUNTABILITY

If you are always seen, you are also always accountable. Your actions have consequences, and those consequences are witnessed. You cannot escape into anonymity or denial. This might sound oppressive, but it is actually clarifying. It means your choices matter. Your actions have weight. Your life has significance.

In a universe where no one is watching, where nothing matters, where all actions disappear into meaningless void, there is no accountability and therefore no meaning. But in a universe where everything is seen, where every action is witnessed, where nothing is lost or forgotten, your choices have eternal significance.

This does not mean you should live in fear of judgment. Remember: the Architect sees you with love, not condemnation. The divine gaze is not a harsh judge looking for reasons to punish but a loving parent watching a child learn and grow.

But it does mean you should live with awareness of the weight of your choices. It means recognizing that how you treat others matters, that what you do with your time and energy matters, that the kind of person you are becoming matters.

Living from accountability means taking responsibility for your actions and their consequences. It means acknowledging when you have caused harm and making amends. It means learning from your mistakes rather than denying them. It means growing in wisdom and compassion rather than remaining stuck in destructive patterns. This is part of the curriculum of the classroom. You are learning to be the kind of being who can participate in the eternal reward, who can exist in direct relationship with the Architect. And that requires developing character, integrity, wisdom, love.

The fact that you are always seen helps you develop these qualities. It keeps you honest. It prevents you from deceiving yourself. It reminds you that your life has meaning and purpose.

LIVING FROM CONFIDENCE

We explored confidence in Chapter 5, but it is worth returning to here. Confidence, in the deepest sense, is not arrogance or self-assertion. It is the quiet assurance that comes from knowing you are held, known, loved by the Architect.

When you live as though you are seen—because you are seen—you can act with confidence. Not because you are perfect, but because you are accepted. Not because you have all the answers, but because you are guided. Not because you are in control, but because you trust the one who is.

This confidence allows you to take risks, to try new things, to step into the unknown. Because you know that even if you fail, even if you make mistakes, even if you fall flat on your face, you are still seen, still known, still loved. This confidence allows you to be generous, to give freely, to serve others. Because you know that your worth does not depend on what you achieve or accumulate. You are already valuable, already significant, already enough.

This confidence allows you to be humble, to acknowledge your limitations, to ask for help. Because you do not need to pretend to be more than you are. You can be honest about your weaknesses, knowing that they do not diminish your worth.

This confidence allows you to be present, to engage fully with life, to show up authentically in each moment. Because you are not worried about managing perceptions or protecting your image. You can simply be who you are, where you are, doing what you are doing.

Living from confidence is living from the truth of your relationship with the Architect. It is living as though you are seen—because you are. It is living as though you are known—because you are. It is living as though you are loved—because you are.

THE PRACTICE OF REMEMBERING

The challenge is that we forget. We forget that we are seen. We forget that we are known. We forget that we are loved. We slip back into the old patterns of hiding, pretending, performing. We act as though we are alone, as though no one is watching, as though our choices do not matter.

This is why we need practice. We need regular reminders of the truth. We need disciplines that help us remember.

Prayer is one such discipline. When you pray, you are acknowledging the presence of the Architect. You are speaking to the one who sees you, knows you, loves you. You are remembering that you are not alone.

Meditation is another. When you sit in silence, you create space to feel the presence that is always there. You quiet the noise of the mind and open yourself to the awareness of being witnessed.

Scripture or sacred texts can serve this function. When you read words that point to the divine reality, you are reminded of truths you tend to forget. You are reorienting yourself to the larger context of your existence.

Community is important too. When you gather with others who are also seeking to live consciously, to remember the truth, to align with the Architect's purposes, you support each other in the practice of remembering. And simple mindfulness throughout the day can help. Pausing periodically to remember: I am seen. I am known. I am loved. Taking a breath and feeling the presence of the Architect. Bringing your awareness back to the truth of your existence.

These practices are not about earning the Architect's love or proving your worthiness. They are about remembering what is already true, aligning yourself with the reality that already exists, living from the truth rather than from the illusion.

You are always seen. The question is whether you will live as though you are.

Pause here. Before moving to the next chapter, take a moment to feel what it is like to be seen. Not judged, not evaluated, but simply witnessed with complete love and acceptance.

Can you relax into this seeing? Can you let yourself be known? Can you trust that you are held?

This is the practice. This is the path. This is the way home.

THE PROBLEM OF PARADOX

"Do I contradict myself?
Very well then I contradict myself.
(I am large, I contain multitudes.)"
— Walt Whitman

We have built a comprehensive framework for understanding consciousness, reality, and divine purpose. We have explored the nature of witnessing, the structure of time, the impossibility of hiding, the purpose of suffering, the illusion of separation, and the practice of presence.

But if you have been paying close attention, you may have noticed something troubling: the framework contains contradictions.

We have said that the Block Universe is fixed and predetermined, yet we have also affirmed the reality of free will and meaningful choice. We have said that the Architect knows everything, yet we have also said that we have genuine agency and responsibility. We have said that we are separate individuals, yet we have also said that separation is an illusion and we are fundamentally interconnected.

These are not minor inconsistencies that can be resolved with better definitions or clearer thinking. These are genuine paradoxes—statements that seem to contradict each other yet both appear to be true.

For many people, paradox is a problem to be solved. We want our worldview to be logically consistent, our beliefs to fit together neatly, our understanding to be free of contradiction. When we encounter paradox, we try to resolve it, to choose one side or the other, to eliminate the tension.

But what if paradox is not a problem to be solved but a truth to be embraced? What if reality itself contains contradictions that cannot be resolved through logic alone? What if mature spirituality requires learning to hold opposites together without insisting on resolution?

This chapter explores the nature of paradox, why truth contains contradictions, and how to develop the wisdom of both/and.

9.1 WHY TRUTH CONTAINS CONTRADICTIONS

THE LIMITS OF LOGIC

Logic is a powerful tool for understanding reality. It allows us to reason clearly, to identify fallacies, to build coherent arguments, to distinguish truth from falsehood.

But logic has limits. It operates according to certain rules, the most fundamental of which is the law of non-contradiction: a statement cannot be both true and false in the same sense at the same time. Either the ball is blue or it is not blue. Either you have free will or you do not. Either you are separate or you are connected.

This works well for many domains of inquiry. In mathematics, in formal logic, in much of science, the law of non-contradiction is essential. Contradictions indicate errors that need to be corrected.

But when we are dealing with ultimate reality, with the nature of consciousness, with the relationship between time and eternity, with the mystery of divine and human agency—logic begins to break down.

Not because reality is irrational, but because reality is trans-rational. It exceeds the categories of logic. It contains truths that cannot be captured in either/or formulations.

Think of light. Is light a wave or a particle? According to classical physics, it must be one or the other. Waves and particles are fundamentally different kinds of things with incompatible properties.

But quantum mechanics reveals that light is both wave and particle, depending on how you measure it. This is not a failure of understanding or a problem to be solved. This is the nature of light. It exhibits wave-like properties in some contexts and particle-like properties in others. It is both/and, not either/or.

This does not mean that logic is useless or that anything goes. It means that logic is a tool with a specific domain of application, and when we are dealing with realities that transcend that domain, we need different tools, different ways of knowing.

THE LIMITS OF LANGUAGE

Language, like logic, has limits. Words are symbols that point to realities beyond themselves. They are useful for communication, for thinking, for organizing experience.

But words are also reductive. They take the infinite complexity of reality and reduce it to discrete categories. They create boundaries, distinctions, separations.

This is necessary and useful. We could not think or communicate without language. But it also means that language inevitably distorts reality, especially when we are trying to describe realities that transcend ordinary experience.

How do you describe the taste of honey to someone who has never tasted it? You can use analogies—"It is sweet like sugar but with a floral quality"—but the words can never capture the actual experience. The reality exceeds the description.

Similarly, how do you describe the nature of consciousness, the experience of the divine, the relationship between time and eternity? You can use metaphors, analogies, poetic language, but the words always fall short. The reality exceeds the description.

This is why spiritual traditions across cultures use paradoxical language. The Tao that can be spoken is not the eternal Tao. God is both transcendent and immanent, both beyond all things and present in all things. The self must be lost to be found. You must die to live.

These are not logical contradictions to be resolved. They are pointers to realities that transcend the either/or categories of ordinary language. They are invitations to a different kind of knowing, a knowing that embraces mystery and paradox.

THE NATURE OF ULTIMATE REALITY

Why does ultimate reality contain paradoxes? Why can it not be captured in logically consistent propositions?

One reason is that ultimate reality is infinite, and the infinite cannot be fully grasped by the finite mind. We are limited beings trying to understand unlimited reality. Our concepts, our categories, our logical structures—all of these are finite tools trying to grasp the infinite.

It is like trying to contain the ocean in a cup. You can scoop up some water, and that water is real ocean water, but it is not the ocean. The ocean exceeds the cup. Similarly, our concepts can capture aspects of ultimate reality, but they cannot contain it.

Another reason is that ultimate reality is unified, and unity transcends the distinctions that language and logic require. Language works by making distinctions—this versus that, subject versus object, self versus other. But ultimate reality is the ground of all distinctions, the unity that precedes and includes all differences.

When we try to describe this unity using the tools of distinction, we inevitably create paradoxes. We say that all is one, yet many things exist. We say that God is beyond all things, yet present in all things. We say that the self is an illusion, yet the self is real.

These paradoxes arise not because we are confused but because we are trying to use the language of distinction to describe the reality of unity.

A third reason is that ultimate reality includes both the temporal and the eternal, both the relative and the absolute, both the perspective of the finite being and the perspective of the infinite consciousness.

From the temporal perspective, you are a separate individual making choices in time. From the eternal perspective, you are a pattern in the Block Universe, part of the unified consciousness that grounds all reality.

Both perspectives are true. But they seem to contradict each other because they are describing reality from different vantage points. The contradiction is not in reality but in our attempt to reconcile perspectives that cannot be fully reconciled through logic alone.

PARADOX AS INVITATION

When we encounter paradox, we have a choice. We can see it as a problem that indicates confusion or error, something to be resolved or eliminated. Or we can see it as an invitation to a deeper understanding, a pointer to realities that transcend our ordinary ways of knowing.

The first response keeps us within the limits of logic and language. It is safe, comfortable, familiar. But it also keeps us from the deeper truths that paradox points toward.

The second response requires us to venture beyond the limits of logic and language. It is uncomfortable, disorienting, challenging. But it opens us to the mystery, to the infinite, to the realities that cannot be captured in neat formulations.

Mature spirituality requires the second response. It requires learning to sit with paradox, to hold contradictions without resolving them, to embrace mystery without demanding answers.

This does not mean abandoning reason or embracing irrationality. It means recognizing that reason is a tool with limits, and that some truths can only be known through direct experience, through contemplation, through the kind of knowing that transcends conceptual understanding. Paradox is not a failure of understanding. It is an invitation to a different kind of understanding, a knowing that includes but transcends logic, a wisdom that can hold opposites together in creative tension.

9.2 HOLDING OPPOSITES WITHOUT RESOLUTION

THE DISCOMFORT OF PARADOX

Holding opposites without resolution is deeply uncomfortable for most people. We want clarity, certainty, consistency. We want to know which side is right so we can commit to it fully.

When we encounter paradox, we feel cognitive dissonance—the psychological discomfort that arises when we hold contradictory beliefs. Our minds want to resolve the dissonance, to choose one side or the other, to eliminate the contradiction.

This is a natural response. Our brains are wired to seek patterns, to create coherent narratives, to organize information into consistent frameworks. Contradiction threatens this coherence, and we instinctively try to restore it.

But what if the discomfort is not a sign that something is wrong but a sign that we are approaching truth? What if the tension of paradox is precisely what we need to hold in order to grasp realities that transcend either/or thinking? Think of the paradox of free will and determinism. If you choose one side—pure free will—you lose the insights of the Block Universe, the recognition that all moments exist simultaneously, the understanding that your life is a complete pattern in the fabric of spacetime.

If you choose the other side—pure determinism—you lose the reality of your subjective experience, the genuine feeling of choice, the moral responsibility that comes with agency.

But if you hold both sides together, if you embrace the paradox, you can access a deeper truth: that free will and determinism are not contradictory but complementary, two perspectives on the same reality, both true from different vantage points.

This requires tolerating the discomfort of not having a neat resolution. It requires living with the tension, holding the opposites in creative balance, resisting the urge to collapse the paradox into a simpler either/or.

THE PRACTICE OF BOTH/AND

How do we develop the capacity to hold opposites without resolution? How do we move from either/or thinking to both/and wisdom?

First, we must recognize when we are engaging in either/or thinking. Notice when you find yourself saying "It is either this or that." Notice when you feel the need to choose sides, to declare one perspective right and the other wrong.

This either/or thinking is often a defense against complexity, a way of simplifying reality so it feels more manageable. But reality is not simple. Reality is complex, multifaceted, paradoxical.

Second, we must practice holding both sides of a paradox simultaneously. This is a mental discipline, like holding two objects in your hands at once. You do not drop one to pick up the other. You hold both.

Take the paradox of divine omniscience and human freedom. God knows everything, including all your future choices. Yet you experience yourself as free, as genuinely choosing, as responsible for your actions.

Instead of trying to resolve this paradox—by denying either God's omniscience or human freedom—practice holding both truths together. God knows all your choices, and you are genuinely free. Both are true. The paradox is real.

Sit with this. Feel the tension. Notice the discomfort. Do not try to resolve it. Just hold it.

As you practice this, something shifts. The either/or categories begin to loosen. The need for resolution begins to fade. You develop a capacity to hold complexity, to embrace mystery, to live with questions that have no simple answers.

Third, we must cultivate humility about the limits of our understanding. Paradox reminds us that we do not have all the answers, that reality exceeds our comprehension, that mystery is real.

This humility is not a weakness but a strength. It opens us to learning, to growth, to the possibility that there are truths we have not yet grasped. It keeps us from the arrogance of thinking we have figured everything out.

Fourth, we must learn to think in terms of perspectives rather than absolute truths. Many paradoxes arise because we are trying to reconcile different perspectives on the same reality.

From the perspective of eternity, the Block Universe is fixed and complete. From the perspective of time, the future is open and your choices matter. Both perspectives are valid. The paradox arises when we try to collapse them into a single perspective.

Learning to shift between perspectives, to see reality from multiple vantage points, to recognize that different perspectives reveal different different aspects of truth—this is a key skill in holding paradox.

EXAMPLES OF PARADOX IN SPIRITUAL LIFE

Let us explore some specific paradoxes that arise in spiritual life and practice holding them without resolution.

Transcendence and Immanence: God is utterly transcendent, beyond all things, infinite and eternal, wholly other. And God is utterly immanent, present in all things, closer to you than your own breath, the ground of your being.

Both are true. God is not partly transcendent and partly immanent. God is fully both. The paradox is real.

How do you hold this? By recognizing that transcendence and immanence are not opposites but complementary aspects of the divine nature. God is beyond all things precisely because God is the ground of all things. The infinite transcends the finite by being present in it.

Effort and Grace: Spiritual growth requires tremendous effort—discipline, practice, commitment, struggle. And spiritual growth is entirely a gift of grace—you cannot earn it, achieve it, or make it happen through your own power.

Both are true. You must work as though everything depends on you, and you must trust as though everything depends on God. How do you hold this? By recognizing that your effort is itself a gift of grace, that the desire to grow is planted in you by the Architect, that your striving and God's giving are not separate but two aspects of the same movement.

Self and No-Self: You are a real, unique individual with particular gifts, perspectives, and purposes. And the separate self is an illusion, a temporary construction that will dissolve, revealing your fundamental unity with all things.

Both are true. You are a distinct pattern in the web of reality, and you are inseparable from the web.

How do you hold this? By recognizing that individuality and unity are not contradictory but complementary. You are a unique expression of the one reality. Your individuality is real precisely because it is a particular manifestation of the universal.

Suffering and Love: The universe contains tremendous suffering—pain, loss, injustice, tragedy. And the universe is created and sustained by infinite love, by an Architect who cares for every being with perfect compassion.

Both are true. The suffering is real, and the love is real.

How do you hold this? By recognizing that love does not eliminate suffering but transforms it, that the Architect does not prevent all pain but accompanies us through it, that suffering can be a teacher and love can be present even in the midst of agony.

These paradoxes cannot be resolved through logic. They can only be held, contemplated, lived with. And as you practice holding them, you develop a different kind of wisdom—a wisdom that can embrace mystery, that can live with questions, that can find truth in the tension between opposites.

THE WISDOM OF UNKNOWING

There is a long tradition in Christian mysticism called apophatic theology or the via negativa—the way of negation. This approach recognizes that God is ultimately beyond all concepts, all descriptions, all categories.

We can say what God is not more accurately than we can say what God is. God is not limited, not finite, not changing, not material. But when we try to say what God is, our words inevitably fall short.

This leads to a practice of unknowing—letting go of concepts, releasing the need to understand, opening to the mystery that exceeds all comprehension.

This is not ignorance. It is a sophisticated form of knowing, a recognition that the deepest truths cannot be grasped by the conceptual mind but can only be experienced directly, in silence, in contemplation, in the space beyond words.

Paradox invites us into this unknowing. When we encounter contradictions that cannot be resolved, when we reach the limits of logic and language, we are invited to let go of the need to understand and simply be present to the mystery.

This is uncomfortable for the rational mind. The mind wants to know, to understand, to have clear answers. But the heart can rest in mystery. The heart can be present to what exceeds comprehension.

Learning to hold paradox is learning to trust the heart's knowing over the mind's need for certainty. It is learning to be comfortable with not knowing, to find peace in the questions, to embrace the mystery.

9.3 THE WISDOM OF BOTH/AND

BEYOND DUALISTIC THINKING

Most of our ordinary thinking is dualistic. We divide reality into opposites: good and bad, right and wrong, self and other, sacred and profane, spiritual and material.

This dualistic thinking is useful for navigating everyday life. It helps us make decisions, set boundaries, organize experience. But it also distorts reality, creating false separations, missing the deeper unity that underlies apparent opposites.

The wisdom of both/and is the wisdom that transcends dualism without denying distinctions. It recognizes that opposites are often complementary rather than contradictory, that reality includes both poles of apparent contradictions, that truth is found not in choosing one side but in holding both.

This is not the same as saying "everything is relative" or "all perspectives are equally valid." Some things are true and some are false. Some actions are right and some are wrong. Distinctions matter.

But the wisdom of both/and recognizes that many of the opposites we perceive are not absolute contradictions but different aspects of a larger whole, different perspectives on a unified reality, different expressions of the same truth.

Light is both wave and particle. You are both individual and interconnected. God is both transcendent and immanent. The universe is both determined and free. Spiritual growth requires both effort and grace.

These are not compromises or middle positions. They are recognitions that reality is richer, more complex, more paradoxical than either/or thinking can capture.

THE COINCIDENCE OF OPPOSITES

There is a concept in Christian mysticism, articulated by Nicholas of Cusa, called the *coincidentia oppositorum*—the coincidence of opposites. This is the idea that in God, all opposites are reconciled, all contradictions are resolved, all paradoxes are held in perfect unity.

God is both infinite and intimate, both unchanging and responsive, both one and many, both beyond all things and present in all things. In God, these opposites do not contradict but coincide, existing together in perfect harmony.

We, as finite beings, cannot fully grasp this coincidence of opposites. We experience reality from a limited perspective, and from that perspective, opposites seem contradictory. But as we grow in spiritual maturity, as we expand our consciousness, as we approach the divine perspective, we begin to see how opposites can coincide.

This is not something we can achieve through intellectual effort alone. It requires contemplation, meditation, direct experience of the divine reality. It requires moving beyond the conceptual mind into the space of mystical knowing.

But we can practice it. We can practice holding opposites together, noticing when they coincide, recognizing the unity that underlies apparent contradiction.

When you are fully present, time and eternity coincide. The present moment is both a fleeting instant in the flow of time and a doorway to the eternal now.

When you are fully loving, self and other coincide. You give yourself away and find yourself more fully. You serve the other and discover your own deepest fulfillment.

When you are fully surrendered, effort and grace coincide. You work with all your strength and trust completely in God. Your striving and God's giving are one movement.

These moments of coincidence are glimpses of the divine reality, tastes of the wisdom that transcends dualism, experiences of the both/ and that holds all opposites in unity.

PRACTICAL APPLICATIONS

How does the wisdom of both/and apply to practical life? How does it change how we live, how we make decisions, how we relate to others?

First, it makes us more humble and less dogmatic. When we recognize that truth often includes both sides of apparent contradictions, we become less certain that we have all the answers, less quick to judge others who see things differently, more open to learning and growth.

This does not mean we abandon our convictions or become wishy-washy. It means we hold our convictions with humility, recognizing that our perspective is limited, that others may see aspects of truth that we have missed, that reality is more complex than any single viewpoint can capture.

Second, it makes us more compassionate and less judgmental. When we recognize that people contain multitudes, that they can be both good and flawed, both wounded and resilient, both selfish and generous, we become less quick to categorize them as simply good or bad.

We can hold the complexity of human nature, recognizing that the same person can act with great kindness in one moment and great cruelty in another, that people are not fixed categories but dynamic processes, that everyone is on a journey of growth and learning.

Third, it makes us more creative and less rigid in problem-solving. When we move beyond either/or thinking, we open up new possibilities. Instead of asking "Should we do A or B?" we can ask "How can we do both A and B?" or "What third option includes the best of both?"

This both/and thinking is essential for addressing complex problems that do not have simple solutions. How do we balance individual freedom and collective responsibility? How do we honor both justice and mercy? How do we pursue both economic growth and environmental sustainability?

These are not either/or questions. They require both/and wisdom, the capacity to hold multiple values in creative tension, to find solutions that honor complexity rather than reducing it to false simplicity.

Fourth, it makes us more integrated and less fragmented. When we stop dividing reality into rigid opposites, we can integrate aspects of ourselves that we have kept separate.

We can be both strong and vulnerable, both confident and humble, both serious and playful. We can honor both our need for solitude and our need for community, both our spiritual aspirations and our earthly responsibilities, both our individual uniqueness and our fundamental interconnection.

This integration is the path to wholeness, to becoming fully human, to embodying the both/and wisdom that reflects the divine nature.

THE ULTIMATE BOTH/AND

The ultimate both/and is the relationship between the human and the divine, the finite and the infinite, the temporal and the eternal.

You are both a limited, mortal being living in time and an eternal expression of infinite consciousness. You are both a separate individual and inseparable from the whole. You are both a student in the classroom and a beloved child of the Architect.

This is the great paradox of human existence. We are both/and. We are creatures and creators, finite and infinite, temporal and eternal, separate and united.

And the spiritual journey is the journey of learning to hold this paradox, to live from both sides of it, to be fully human and fully divine, fully in time and fully in eternity, fully individual and fully interconnected.

This is what the Architect is teaching you. This is what the classroom is for. This is the wisdom that prepares you for the eternal reward.

You cannot resolve the paradox. You can only live it. You can only be it. You can only surrender to the mystery and trust that the Architect holds all contradictions in perfect unity. And as you practice this surrender, as you learn to hold opposites without resolution, as you develop the wisdom of both/and, you discover something remarkable:

The paradox is not a problem. The paradox is the truth. The paradox is the doorway to the divine.

Pause here. Before moving to the final chapter, sit with the paradoxes of your own life. What opposites are you trying to reconcile? What contradictions are you trying to resolve?

What if you stopped trying to resolve them? What if you simply held them, honored them, lived them?

This is the wisdom the Architect is offering you. This is the both/and that leads to wholeness. Are you ready to embrace it?

PART IV

THE RETURN

THE RETURN

> "The end of all our exploring
> will be to arrive where we started
> and know the place
> for the first time."
> — T.S. Eliot

We have journeyed far together. We have explored the nature of consciousness and reality, the structure of time and eternity, the impossibility of hiding from divine omniscience, the purpose of suffering, the illusion of separation, the practice of presence, and the wisdom of paradox.

But a journey is not complete until you return home. And the spiritual journey is ultimately a journey of return—a return to your true nature, a return to your source, a return to the Architect who created you and has been calling you home all along.

This final chapter is about that return. It is about the stages of spiritual maturation, the recognition that the map is not the territory, and the ultimate homecoming to the Architect.

10.1 STAGES OF SPIRITUAL MATURATION

THE JOURNEY HAS STAGES

Spiritual growth is not a linear progression from ignorance to enlightenment, from darkness to light, from separation to union. It is more like a spiral, circling back to the same themes at deeper levels, revisiting the same questions with greater wisdom, returning to the same truths with fresh understanding.

But there are recognizable stages in this journey, patterns that many seekers experience, milestones that mark progress along the path. Understanding these stages can help you recognize where you are, what challenges you are facing, and what lies ahead. Different traditions map these stages differently. Christianity speaks of purgation, illumination, and union. Buddhism speaks of stream-entry, once-returning, non-returning, and arhatship. Sufism speaks of the stations and states of the path. Hinduism speaks of the stages of yoga.

The specific maps vary, but they point to similar realities: there are phases of awakening, phases of purification, phases of deepening understanding, phases of integration, and ultimately, phases of union with the divine.

What follows is one way of mapping these stages, drawing on multiple traditions but adapted to the framework we have been developing throughout this book.

STAGE ONE: THE SLEEP OF UNCONSCIOUSNESS

The first stage is not really a stage of the spiritual journey but the state from which the journey begins. This is the state of unconscious living, of sleepwalking through life, of being completely identified with the ego and its concerns.

In this stage, you are not aware that you are asleep. You take the illusion of separation for granted. You believe that you are a separate, isolated self, that the material world is all there is, that your purpose is to pursue pleasure and avoid pain, to accumulate possessions and achievements, to secure your position in the social hierarchy.

You may be successful by worldly standards. You may have wealth, status, relationships, accomplishments. But there is an underlying sense of dissatisfaction, a vague feeling that something is missing, a hunger that worldly success cannot satisfy.

This is the state that most people live in most of the time. It is not a moral failing. It is simply the default condition of human consciousness in a culture that does not prioritize spiritual awakening.

The transition out of this stage usually comes through some kind of disruption—a crisis, a loss, a moment of profound questioning. Something happens that cracks the shell of unconsciousness and allows the light to get in.

STAGE TWO: THE AWAKENING

The second stage is the initial awakening, the first recognition that there is more to reality than the material world, that you are more than your ego, that there is a spiritual dimension to existence.

This awakening can come in many forms. It might be a mystical experience, a moment of profound peace or connection or insight. It might be an intellectual realization, a sudden understanding of a spiritual truth. It might be an encounter with a teacher, a text, a practice that opens your eyes to new possibilities.

However it comes, the awakening is characterized by a sense of discovery, of seeing something that was always there but that you had never noticed before. It is like waking from a dream and realizing that the dream was not reality.

This stage is often accompanied by great enthusiasm and energy. You have discovered something precious, and you want to explore it, to understand it, to share it with others. You may dive into spiritual practices, read voraciously, seek out teachers and communities.

But this stage also has its challenges. The initial awakening is often followed by a period of confusion and disorientation. The old certainties have been shaken, but new certainties have not yet formed. You are between worlds, no longer fully identified with the ego but not yet established in a deeper identity.

There can also be a tendency toward spiritual pride in this stage. You have seen something that others have not seen, and you may feel superior to those who are still asleep. You may become judgmental, dismissive of those who do not share your newfound insights.

This is a natural but problematic response. True spiritual awakening leads to humility, not pride; to compassion, not judgment. If your awakening is making you arrogant, it is a sign that you are still operating from the ego, just with a spiritual veneer.

STAGE THREE: THE DARK NIGHT

The third stage is what mystics call the dark night of the soul—a period of profound difficulty, doubt, and disillusionment that often follows the initial awakening.

In this stage, the enthusiasm of the awakening fades. The practices that once brought joy and insight now feel dry and empty. The sense of connection to the divine that once felt so real now seems distant or absent. You may feel abandoned by God, lost in darkness, unsure whether any of it was real.

This is one of the most difficult stages of the spiritual journey, and many people get stuck here or turn back. It feels like failure, like you have lost what you once had, like you are going backward rather than forward.

But the dark night is not a failure. It is a necessary stage of purification and deepening. The initial awakening often comes with a kind of spiritual consolation, a sense of peace and joy that makes the path feel easy and pleasant. But this consolation is a gift for beginners, not the final destination.

The dark night strips away the consolations, the pleasant feelings, the sense of progress and achievement. It reveals the ways you have been seeking spiritual experiences for your own gratification, using spiritual practices to bolster your ego, clinging to insights as possessions.

In the darkness, you are forced to let go of these attachments. You are forced to seek God for God's sake, not for the feelings or experiences or insights that come with it. You are forced to trust when you cannot see, to continue when you feel nothing, to surrender when you have no sense of control.

This is the crucible of transformation. What emerges from the dark night is a deeper, more mature faith—a faith that does not depend on feelings or experiences, a faith that can endure doubt and difficulty, a faith that is rooted not in what you get from God but in who God is.

The dark night is also a death—a death of the ego, a death of the false self, a death of the illusion of separation. And like all deaths, it is painful. But it is also necessary. You must die to the old self in order to be born into the new.

STAGE FOUR: ILLUMINATION AND UNDERSTANDING

The fourth stage is illumination—a period of deepening understanding, clarity, and insight that follows the dark night.

In this stage, the darkness lifts. Not all at once, but gradually. You begin to see with new eyes, to understand with new depth, to perceive realities that were hidden before.

The truths you encountered in the initial awakening return, but now they are not just ideas or experiences—they are lived realities. You do not just know about the interconnection of all things; you experience it directly. You do not just believe in divine omniscience; you feel yourself held in the divine gaze.

This stage is characterized by a sense of integration. The paradoxes that once seemed contradictory now reveal their deeper unity. The practices that once felt like obligations now feel like natural expressions of your being. The teachings that once seemed abstract now make perfect sense in light of your experience.

There is also a deepening of compassion in this stage. Having passed through the dark night, having faced your own darkness and been transformed by it, you develop a profound empathy for others who are suffering. You recognize that everyone is on a journey, that everyone is doing the best they can with the understanding they have, that judgment is inappropriate and compassion is the only fitting response.

This stage can last for years or even decades. It is a time of steady growth, of deepening practice, of increasing alignment with the divine will. It is not without challenges—there may be smaller dark nights, periods of difficulty and doubt—but the overall trajectory is one of growth and maturation.

STAGE FIVE: UNION AND SERVICE

The fifth stage is union—the experience of fundamental oneness with the divine, the dissolution of the sense of separation, the realization of your true nature as an expression of infinite consciousness.

This is not a permanent state that you achieve once and for all. It is more like a deepening capacity to rest in the truth of union, to live from that truth even in the midst of ordinary life.

In this stage, the distinction between sacred and profane dissolves. Everything becomes a manifestation of the divine. Every moment becomes an opportunity for worship. Every action becomes an expression of love.

There is a profound sense of freedom in this stage—not the freedom to do whatever you want, but the freedom from the tyranny of the ego, from the compulsion to protect and promote the separate self. You are free to be who you truly are, to respond to each moment with authenticity and love.

This stage is also characterized by a natural movement toward service. When you experience union with the divine, you simultaneously experience union with all beings. Their suffering becomes your suffering. Their joy becomes your joy. And so compassion arises naturally, not as a moral obligation but as a spontaneous expression of your true nature.

Service in this stage is not about self-sacrifice in the conventional sense. It is not about denying your own needs to meet the needs of others. Rather, it is about recognizing that there is no fundamental distinction between self and other, between your flourishing and the flourishing of the whole.

When you serve from this place, there is no sense of burden or resentment. You give freely because giving is an expression of who you are. You receive freely because you recognize that everything is gift. The distinction between giving and receiving begins to blur.

This is what the mystics mean when they speak of becoming a "hollow reed" or an "empty vessel" through which divine love flows. You are not the source of the love—the Architect is the source. But you are the channel, the expression, the particular form that love takes in this moment, in this place, with this person.

Union does not mean the end of your individuality. You do not dissolve into an undifferentiated cosmic soup. Rather, you become more fully yourself—the unique expression of divine consciousness that you were always meant to be. Your gifts, your personality, your particular way of seeing and being in the world—all of this remains and is sanctified, offered back to the Architect in service.

THE SPIRAL NATURE OF GROWTH

It is important to understand that these stages are not strictly linear. Spiritual growth is more like a spiral than a ladder. You may touch union briefly in the awakening stage, then spend years in purification. You may cycle through dark nights multiple times, each one deeper than the last. You may experience moments of profound illumination followed by periods of ordinary consciousness.

This is normal. This is the way the path works. Do not judge yourself for "going backward" or "losing ground." You are not losing ground. You are spiraling deeper into the truth, and sometimes that requires revisiting territory you thought you had already covered.

Each time you return to a familiar challenge or question, you bring more wisdom, more capacity, more depth. The spiral is not a circle—you are not simply repeating the same experience. You are encountering it from a new level of understanding. Trust the process. Trust that the Architect knows what you need and when you need it. Trust that your particular path, with all its twists and turns and apparent detours, is exactly the path you need to walk.

BEYOND THE STAGES

Finally, we must acknowledge that these stages are themselves a map, not the territory. They are a useful framework for understanding spiritual growth, but they are not the reality itself.

Some people will recognize their own experience in these stages. Others will find that their journey looks quite different. Both are valid. The Architect works with each person according to their unique nature and needs.

The point is not to identify which stage you are in so you can feel proud or discouraged. The point is to recognize that spiritual growth is real, that transformation is possible, that the path leads somewhere.

And where does it lead? It leads home. It leads to the Architect. It leads to the realization that you were never separate, never lost, never alone. It leads to the truth that has been waiting for you all along.

10.2 THE MAP IS NOT THE TERRITORY

THE LIMITS OF LANGUAGE

We have traveled together through ten chapters, exploring consciousness and reality, determinism and free will, divine knowledge and human secrets, suffering and grace, separation and union. We have used metaphors—the void and the witness, the Block Universe, the box, the classroom, the web of consciousness, the return.

These metaphors have been useful. They have pointed toward truths that are difficult to express in ordinary language. They have created frameworks for understanding experiences that often feel ineffable.

But now we must acknowledge something crucial: the map is not the territory.

All of these concepts, all of these metaphors, all of these carefully constructed arguments—they are fingers pointing at the moon, not the moon itself. They are maps of a territory that must ultimately be explored directly, not through description but through experience.

This is not a failure of the book or of language itself. It is simply the nature of ultimate reality. The divine cannot be captured in concepts. The truth of your being cannot be fully expressed in words. The experience of union cannot be conveyed through metaphor, no matter how skillful. Language operates through distinction and separation. We create meaning by drawing boundaries—this is a tree, that is a rock; this is self, that is other; this is sacred, that is profane. Language is inherently dualistic.

But ultimate reality is non-dual. It is the unified ground from which all distinctions arise. It is the consciousness that precedes and transcends all categories. And so any attempt to describe it in language will necessarily fall short.

This does not mean we should abandon language or concepts. They are useful tools. They can point us in the right direction. They can help us recognize truth when we encounter it directly. They can provide frameworks for integrating our experiences.

But we must hold them lightly. We must not mistake the description for the reality. We must not cling to the map when we need to walk the territory.

THE DANGER OF CONCEPTUAL UNDERSTANDING

There is a particular danger for those who are intellectually inclined, who love ideas and frameworks and systematic understanding. The danger is that we can become so enamored with the map that we never actually take the journey.

We can read books about meditation without ever sitting in silence. We can study theories of consciousness without ever examining our own awareness. We can discuss the nature of divine love without ever opening our hearts to receive it.

This is what Zen Buddhists call "stinking of Zen"—having all the right concepts and vocabulary without any genuine realization. It is what Christians warn against when they speak of knowledge that "puffs up" rather than builds up.

Conceptual understanding has its place. It can prepare the ground. It can remove obstacles. It can give us confidence to take the next step. But it cannot substitute for direct experience.

You can read this entire book, understand every argument, appreciate every metaphor, and still not know the truth it points toward. Knowledge about the divine is not the same as knowledge of the divine. Description of union is not the same as the experience of union.

At some point, you must put down the book. You must close your eyes. You must turn your attention inward. You must be willing to not-know, to rest in uncertainty, to let go of all your concepts and frameworks and simply be present to what is.

This is terrifying for the intellectual mind. The mind wants to understand, to categorize, to control. The mind wants to know where it is going and how to get there. The mind wants a map it can trust.

But the final stages of the journey require you to go beyond the mind. Not to abandon reason—reason has its place—but to recognize its limits. To acknowledge that there are ways of knowing that transcend conceptual understanding.

THE JOURNEY THROUGH THIS BOOK

Let us pause and reflect on the journey we have taken together through these pages.

We began in the void, in darkness, with a simple thought experiment about a blue ball. We explored how consciousness brings reality into being through the act of witnessing. We discovered that you are not a passive observer of a pre-existing world, but an active participant in the ongoing creation of reality.

This was the foundation—the recognition that consciousness matters, that your awareness is not incidental but essential, that the Architect has invited you to turn on the lights and see what has been prepared for you.

From there, we moved to the Block Universe, to the recognition that all moments exist simultaneously in the four-dimensional fabric of spacetime. We grappled with the paradox of determinism and free will, discovering that both are true—the script is written, and yet your choices are genuinely free, genuinely yours.

This challenged our ordinary sense of time and agency. It asked us to hold two seemingly contradictory truths in tension. It introduced us to the wisdom of both/and.

Then we explored the hidden variable, the illusion of secrets, the recognition that the Architect sees all and knows all. We discovered that this total transparency is not a threat but a gift—the freedom to be fully known and fully loved, to drop the exhausting performance of the false self and rest in the truth of who we are.

This was an invitation to honesty, to vulnerability, to the courage of being seen.

We then considered the universe as a classroom, a temporary structure designed to teach us grace. We explored the purpose of limitation, the lessons of suffering, the curriculum of embodied existence. We looked beyond the classroom to the eternal reward—the direct knowledge of the Architect that awaits when the grand illusion of matter dissolves.

This gave us context and purpose. It helped us understand why things are the way they are, why the journey is necessary, where it is leading.

We dove deep into the architecture of suffering, refusing easy answers or cheap comfort. We acknowledged the reality of pain while exploring how suffering can serve as sacred curriculum, refining character and deepening faith.

This was difficult territory. It required us to sit with mystery, to resist the temptation to explain away what cannot be fully explained.

We then examined the illusion of separation, discovering that the boundaries we take for granted—between self and other, between individual and cosmos—are more permeable than we imagine. We explored how witnessing connects all things, how we are expressions of a unified web of consciousness.

We turned to practice—the discipline of presence, the cultivation of attention, the choice to live as though we are seen (because we are). We explored how to become conscious participants rather than unconscious reactors, how to align ourselves with the divine witnessing that grounds all reality.

This made the journey practical. It gave us something to do, a way to engage with these ideas in daily life.

We grappled with paradox, learning to hold opposites without resolution, developing the wisdom of both/and. We discovered that ultimate reality cannot be captured in either/or formulations, that the truth is larger than our categories.

This prepared us for mystery, for the recognition that not everything can be resolved or understood.

And now, in this final chapter, we are exploring the stages of spiritual maturation and preparing for the return—the homecoming to the Architect that is the goal and culmination of the entire journey.

Each chapter has built on what came before. Each concept has prepared the ground for the next. The book has been carefully structured to lead you, step by step, toward a comprehensive vision of reality and your place within it.

But now you must ask yourself: Has this been merely an intellectual exercise? Or has something shifted in you? Have you encountered these ideas only with your mind, or have they touched something deeper—your heart, your soul, your direct experience of being alive?

If the book has remained purely conceptual, then it has failed in its deepest purpose. The goal was never simply to give you new ideas to think about. The goal was to awaken you to the truth of your own being, to help you recognize what you already know at the deepest level, to invite you into direct relationship with the Architect.

GOING BEYOND THE BOOK

So what does it mean to go beyond the book?

It means taking what you have learned and testing it against your own experience. It means not simply believing what you have read, but investigating whether it is true in your own life.

It means developing a practice—meditation, prayer, contemplation, whatever form calls to you—and committing to it with consistency and sincerity.

It means paying attention to your actual experience rather than your ideas about your experience. It means noticing when you are lost in thought versus when you are present to what is. It means cultivating the capacity to witness your own consciousness.

It means being willing to not-know. To rest in uncertainty. To let go of the need to have everything figured out. To trust that the Architect is guiding you even when you cannot see the path.

It means bringing these insights into relationship—with yourself, with others, with the natural world, with the divine. It means allowing your understanding to transform how you live, how you love, how you serve.

It means recognizing that the journey is not about accumulating more knowledge but about becoming more fully who you are. It is not about achieving some future state of enlightenment but about waking up to the truth that is already present.

The book can point you toward this truth. It can remove some obstacles. It can give you language for experiences you may have had but not known how to articulate. It can provide a framework for understanding the spiritual path.

But it cannot walk the path for you. It cannot give you the direct experience of the divine. It cannot substitute for your own practice, your own inquiry, your own willingness to be transformed.

At some point—and perhaps that point is now—you must close the book and open your life. You must stop reading about the journey and actually take it. You must stop thinking about presence and actually be present. You must stop conceptualizing union and actually surrender into it.

This is the invitation that has been implicit throughout these pages. This is the call that has been sounding beneath every argument and metaphor. This is the truth that has been waiting for you to recognize it.

The Architect is not a concept. The Architect is the living reality that grounds your existence, that knows you completely, that loves you infinitely. And the Architect is calling you home. Will you answer?

10.3 COMING HOME TO THE ARCHITECT

THE END OF THE JOURNEY

There is a beautiful paradox at the heart of the spiritual journey: the destination is the starting point. The place you are trying to reach is the place you have never left. The home you are seeking is where you have always been.

This is what T.S. Eliot meant when he wrote: "We shall not cease from exploration, and the end of all our exploring will be to arrive where we started and know the place for the first time."

You began this journey in the void, in darkness, with the question of what makes the ball blue. You explored consciousness and reality, determinism and freedom, knowledge and mystery, suffering and grace, separation and union. You have traveled through complex ideas and challenging paradoxes. You have been asked to hold tensions, to sit with uncertainty, to expand your understanding of who you are and what reality is.

And now, at the end, you discover that you have been circling back to the beginning all along. You have been coming home. But you are not the same person who started this journey. You have been transformed by the exploration. You see with new eyes. You understand with a deeper wisdom. You recognize what was always true but hidden from your awareness.

The ball was always blue, even in the darkness. The Architect was always present, even when you felt alone. You were always held in the infinite consciousness that grounds all reality, even when you believed yourself to be separate and isolated.

The journey has not created these truths. It has revealed them. It has removed the veils that obscured your vision. It has awakened you to what was always already the case.

This is what coming home means. It is not arriving at a new destination but recognizing where you have always been. It is not becoming something you were not but remembering what you have always been. It is not achieving union with the divine but awakening to the union that has never been broken.

THE NATURE OF HOMECOMING

What does it feel like to come home to the Architect?

For some, it is a dramatic experience—a sudden awakening, a moment of clarity so profound that it reorganizes everything. The scales fall from the eyes. The veil is lifted. Reality is seen as it truly is, and nothing is ever the same again.

For others, it is gradual—a slow dawning, a gentle recognition that grows over time. The truth seeps in like water into soil, nourishing roots you did not know you had, bringing forth growth you did not know was possible.

For still others, it is cyclical—moments of profound connection followed by periods of ordinary consciousness, glimpses of home followed by the feeling of exile, experiences of union followed by the return of separation. Each cycle deepens the knowing. Each return home is more complete than the last.

There is no single right way to come home. The Architect meets each person where they are, works with each person according to their unique nature and needs. Your homecoming will be yours alone—as particular and unrepeatable as you are.

But there are some common elements, some shared characteristics of what it means to know yourself as held by the Architect.

There is a sense of profound relief—the relief of finally being able to stop performing, stop pretending, stop trying to earn your place in the universe. You are already home. You have always been home. There is nothing you need to do to deserve it. There is a sense of being known—completely, intimately, without reservation. Every secret is seen. Every wound is witnessed. Every joy is shared. And in this total transparency, there is no shame, only love.

There is a sense of belonging—not just to a community or a tradition, but to reality itself. You are not an accident or an intruder. You are an essential part of the whole, a unique expression of the infinite, a beloved child of the Architect.

There is a sense of purpose—not a specific task or mission (though those may come), but a fundamental orientation toward meaning. Your life matters. Your consciousness matters. Your particular way of witnessing and participating in reality matters.

There is a sense of peace—not the absence of challenge or difficulty, but a deep okayness beneath whatever is happening on the surface. You are held. You are safe. You are home.

And there is a sense of love—vast, unconditional, inexhaustible. The Architect's love for you is not based on your worthiness or your achievements. It is based on your being. You are loved because you are, and nothing can change that.

THE INFINITE NATURE OF HOMECOMING

Here is another paradox: coming home is both a destination and a journey. It is both an arrival and an ongoing process.

You can come home in a moment—in a flash of recognition, in a sudden opening of the heart, in an instant of grace. And in that moment, everything changes. You see the truth. You know yourself as held. You rest in the Architect's love.

But you can also spend a lifetime coming home—deepening your understanding, expanding your capacity, growing in wisdom and compassion and love. Each day brings new opportunities to recognize the truth. Each moment offers a fresh invitation to rest in what is.

This is because the Architect is infinite, and your capacity to know the Architect is always expanding. There is always more to discover, more to understand, more to experience. The homecoming is never complete because the home is infinite.

Think of it like this: Imagine you have been living in a single room of a vast mansion, believing that the room was the entire house. Then one day, a door opens, and you discover there are other rooms—hundreds of them, thousands of them, each one more beautiful than the last. You have come home to the mansion. You are no longer confined to the single room. But you will spend the rest of your life (and beyond) exploring the infinite rooms, discovering new wonders, going deeper into the mystery and beauty of your true home.

This is what the mystics mean when they speak of the infinite nature of God. The Architect is not a finite being that you can fully comprehend. The Architect is the infinite ground of all being, the inexhaustible source of all reality, the eternal mystery that can be known but never exhausted.

And so coming home is both a moment and an eternity. It is both a recognition and an exploration. It is both an arrival and a journey that never ends.

WHAT COMES NEXT

So you have come home. You have recognized the truth of your being. You have awakened to your union with the Architect. What comes next?

Everything and nothing.

Nothing changes in the sense that reality is what it has always been. The Block Universe is still the Block Universe. The laws of physics still operate. You still have a body that gets hungry and tired. You still have relationships that require attention and care. You still have work to do and bills to pay. The external circumstances of your life may not change at all. You may still face the same challenges, the same difficulties, the same mundane tasks that filled your days before.

But everything changes in the sense that you are different. You see differently. You understand differently. You relate differently. You live differently.

You see the sacred in the ordinary. You recognize the divine in the mundane. You experience each moment as an opportunity for worship, each encounter as a meeting with the Architect in disguise.

You live with less fear because you know you are held. You live with less grasping because you know you are provided for. You live with less judgment because you know you are not the judge.

You love more freely because you have been loved freely. You forgive more easily because you have been forgiven. You serve more joyfully because you recognize that service is the natural expression of union.

You hold your opinions more lightly because you know the map is not the territory. You embrace paradox more readily because you have learned the wisdom of both/and. You rest in mystery more comfortably because you trust the Architect even when you cannot see the path. What comes next is the rest of your life, lived from this new place of understanding. What comes next is the ongoing practice of remembering who you are and whose you are. What comes next is the daily choice to live as though you are seen (because you are), to witness reality with full presence, to participate consciously in the ongoing creation of the world.

What comes next is the gradual transformation of everything—your relationships, your work, your sense of purpose, your experience of being alive. Not through dramatic external changes (though those may come), but through the quiet, steady work of living from truth rather than illusion, from love rather than fear, from union rather than separation.

What comes next is the rest of the journey home—because coming home is not a single event but a lifelong practice, a continual returning, a constant remembering.

THE INVITATION

And so we come to the end of this book, which is really a beginning.

You have been given a map. You have been shown a path. You have been offered a vision of reality that includes you as an essential participant, a beloved witness, a unique expression of infinite consciousness. But the map is not the territory. The description is not the experience. The invitation is not the same as the acceptance.

The Architect is calling you home. The Architect has always been calling you home. The Architect will never stop calling you home.

But you must answer. You must turn. You must open your eyes and see what has been prepared for you.

This is not a matter of belief or intellectual assent. This is not about adopting a new philosophy or joining a new tradition. This is about direct recognition of the truth of your being.

You are not separate from the Architect. You have never been separate from the Architect. You cannot be separate from the Architect because the Architect is the ground of your being, the consciousness in which you arise, the love that holds you in existence.

But you can forget this truth. You can live as though you are separate. You can spend your life trying to earn what has already been given, trying to find what you have never lost, trying to become what you have always been.

Or you can remember. You can wake up. You can come home. This is the invitation that has been implicit in every page of this book. This is the call that has been sounding beneath every argument and metaphor. This is the truth that has been waiting for you to recognize it.

The void is not empty—it is full of potential, waiting for your witnessing to bring it into reality.

The Block Universe is not a prison—it is the eternal now in which all moments exist simultaneously, held in the infinite consciousness of the Architect.

The hidden variable is not a threat—it is the freedom of being fully known and fully loved.

The classroom is not a punishment—it is a gift, a carefully designed curriculum to teach you what you need to learn.

The suffering is not meaningless—it is sacred curriculum, refining your character and deepening your capacity for love.

The separation is not real—you are part of the web of consciousness, connected to all things, an expression of the unified whole.

The journey is not about going somewhere else—it is about waking up to where you already are.

And the Architect is not distant or abstract—the Architect is the intimate reality that knows you completely, loves you infinitely, and is calling you home.

Will you answer?

Will you turn your attention inward and see what is there?

Will you open your heart and receive the love that has always been offered?

Will you recognize yourself as the witness, the beloved, the one who has never been separate?

Will you come home?

I encourage you to take these pauses seriously. Spiritual understanding is not merely intellectual assent; it is a transformation of consciousness that requires time and stillness.

Finally, I want to address the question you may already be asking: "Is this book true?"

The answer is both simpler and more complex than you might expect. The metaphors and frameworks presented here are models—ways of pointing toward realities that exceed our capacity for direct description. The map is not the territory. The menu is not the meal. But a good map can guide you toward the territory, and a good menu can help you order the meal.

What I can promise you is this: if you engage with these ideas sincerely, if you allow them to challenge and expand your understanding, you will not finish this book as the same person who began it. The movie does not change, but the movie changes you.

The Architect is waiting. The classroom is in session.

The lights are ready to be turned on.

Let us begin.

With hope and humility, Toney James

DISCUSSION QUESTIONS FOR SPIRITUAL GROUPS

These questions are designed to facilitate deep, authentic conversation in spiritual study groups, book clubs, or personal reflection. There are no "correct" answers. The goal is to engage honestly with the material and with your own experience, to listen deeply to others, and to remain open to new understanding.

CONSCIOUSNESS AND REALITY (CHAPTERS 1-2)

In the thought experiment of the blue ball in darkness, the book suggests that consciousness "makes things real" through the act of witnessing. How does this idea sit with you? Can you think of experiences in your own life where your awareness seemed to bring something into fuller reality?

The Block Universe presents all moments as existing simultaneously, with free will as the subjective experience within an objective predetermined framework. How do you hold the tension between determinism and freedom in your own life? Does this framework help or hinder your sense of agency and responsibility?

DIVINE KNOWLEDGE AND WITNESSING (CHAPTER 3)

Chapter 3 explores the idea that nothing can be hidden from the Architect—that all secrets are known, all deceptions are seen. Does this feel threatening or liberating to you? How might your life change if you truly lived as though you were completely known and completely loved?

The book suggests that the "beginning of wisdom" is recognizing that we cannot hide from divine truth. What role does honesty—with yourself, with others, with the divine—play in your spiritual life? Where do you still feel the need to hide or perform?

PURPOSE AND GRACE (CHAPTERS 4-5)

The universe is described as a "classroom" designed to teach grace, with physical reality as temporary scaffolding for spiritual development. Does this metaphor resonate with your experience? What lessons do you think you are meant to learn in this lifetime?

Chapter 5 presents the Architect's love as the fundamental motivation for creation—the universe exists because "love creates." How does this understanding of divine purpose differ from other frameworks you have encountered? How does it affect your sense of meaning and belonging?

SUFFERING (CHAPTER 6)

The book refuses to offer simple explanations for suffering, instead exploring how pain can serve as "sacred curriculum." What has suffering taught you? Are there experiences of pain in your life that you can now see as having contributed to your growth or deepening?

Chapter 6 suggests that some suffering has no inherent meaning but can be given meaning through how we respond to it. How do you distinguish between suffering that should be accepted and suffering that should be resisted or changed? What role does discernment play in your spiritual practice?

INTERCONNECTION (CHAPTER 7)

The illusion of separation is challenged through the metaphor of Indra's Net and the web of consciousness. In what ways do you experience yourself as separate? In what ways do you experience yourself as connected? How might your life change if you lived more fully from the recognition of interconnection?

The book suggests that "the other's suffering is your suffering, the other's joy is your joy." How do you practice this kind of radical empathy? What are the challenges and gifts of recognizing your fundamental unity with all beings?

PRESENCE AND PRACTICE (CHAPTER 8)

Chapter 8 emphasizes the importance of becoming a "conscious participant" rather than living on autopilot. What practices help you cultivate presence in your daily life? What obstacles do you encounter in trying to remain attentive and aware?

The discipline of attention is described as strengthening consciousness like a muscle. Have you experienced this in your own practice? How has your capacity for presence changed over time? What helps you return to awareness when you have been lost in thought or distraction?

PARADOX AND MYSTERY (CHAPTER 9)

The book argues that ultimate reality contains genuine paradoxes that cannot be resolved through logic—we must develop the "wisdom of both/and." What paradoxes do you encounter in your spiritual life? How comfortable are you with holding opposites in tension without resolution?

Chapter 9 suggests that mature spirituality requires embracing mystery rather than demanding certainty. What role does not-knowing play in your spiritual practice? Where do you still cling to the need for definitive answers?

SPIRITUAL MATURATION AND RETURN (CHAPTER 10)

The stages of spiritual maturation described in Chapter 10 include awakening, purification, dark night, illumination, and union. Do you recognize your own journey in these stages? How would you describe where you are now on the spiritual path?

The book ends with the paradox that "the destination is the starting point"—we come home to where we have always been. What does "coming home to the Architect" mean to you? Have you experienced moments of homecoming in your own life? What was that like?

APPENDIX A

KEY METAPHORS EXPLAINED

This appendix provides a reference guide to the central metaphors used throughout the book. Each entry explains the metaphor, why it matters, and how to work with it in your spiritual practice.

THE VOID / DARKNESS

The void or darkness represents the state of physical reality before consciousness observes it—pure potential waiting to be actualized through witnessing. In the thought experiment of the blue ball sealed in a lightless room, the darkness symbolizes how the physical world exists in a kind of silence until a mind speaks its reality into being.

Why it matters: This metaphor challenges our assumption that reality is simply "out there" independent of consciousness. It suggests that awareness is not passive but participative—we are co-creators of reality through the act of witnessing.

How to work with it: Practice noticing the moment when you become aware of something—a sound, a sensation, a thought. Notice how your awareness seems to bring it into fuller reality. Experiment with the question: What exists in your experience before you name it? Can you rest in the unnamed, uninterpreted awareness that precedes conceptual understanding?

THE BLOCK UNIVERSE / THE FILM

The Block Universe is the scientific and philosophical concept that all moments—past, present, and future—exist simultaneously in the four-dimensional fabric of spacetime. The metaphor of a finished film captures this: every frame from beginning to end is already printed on the reel. Your experience of moving through time is like watching the film frame by frame, but the entire movie already exists.

Why it matters: This metaphor addresses the relationship between determinism and free will. It suggests that reality is predetermined (the film is finished) while our experience of choice is genuine (we are watching it unfold). This both/and understanding helps us hold the paradox of freedom within structure.

How to work with it: When facing a difficult decision, try this practice: Imagine that your choice has already been made in the Block Universe. How does this affect your experience of choosing? Does it create fatalism or freedom? Can you choose fully while also trusting that your choice is part of a larger pattern?

THE BOX/THE ILLUSION OF SECRETS

The box represents our belief that we can hide aspects of ourselves from others and from the divine. We imagine our secrets locked away in a container that others cannot access. But the Architect exists "outside the box" and sees all—every thought, every motivation, every hidden wound and secret shame.

Why it matters: This metaphor addresses the exhausting performance of the false self and the freedom that comes from being fully known. When we recognize that we cannot hide from divine truth, we can stop trying to manage our image and rest in authentic being.

How to work with it: Practice radical honesty in your prayer or meditation. Instead of presenting your "best self" to the divine, try showing everything—your doubts, your resentments, your petty thoughts, your shameful desires. Notice what happens when you stop hiding. Does the Architect withdraw? Or does love remain constant?

THE CLASSROOM UNIVERSE

The classroom metaphor presents physical reality as a temporary learning environment designed to teach specific lessons—particularly the lesson of grace. Like a classroom, the universe has structure, curriculum, and purpose. It is not permanent; it is scaffolding that will eventually be removed when the lessons are learned.

Why it matters: This metaphor provides context for suffering, limitation, and the temporary nature of material existence. It suggests that difficulties are not punishments but pedagogy, that constraints serve a purpose, that the physical world is not the final reality.

How to work with it: When facing challenges, try asking: What is this situation trying to teach me? What capacity is being developed? What understanding is being deepened? This doesn't mean every difficulty has a clear lesson, but the question can shift your relationship to hardship from victimhood to curiosity.

THE BEYOND

The Beyond represents the reality that transcends the Block Universe—the eternal realm where direct knowledge replaces mediated understanding, where the relationship with the Architect continues after the dissolution of physical reality. It is "beyond" in the sense of transcending the limitations of space, time, and matter.

Why it matters: This metaphor points toward the eternal reward and the ultimate purpose of existence. It reminds us that the classroom is temporary, that there is more to reality than what we can currently perceive, that death is not the end but a transition.

How to work with it: Practice holding your attachments lightly. When you find yourself clinging to something temporary—a possession, a relationship, a state of being—remind yourself that it is part of the classroom, not the Beyond. This doesn't mean you shouldn't value it, but that you can love it without grasping, enjoy it without demanding it be permanent.

THE ARCHITECT

The Architect is the divine creator who has designed the universe with intention and love. Unlike an abstract or impersonal ultimate reality, the Architect is personal—capable of relationship, knowledge, and love. The Architect exists outside time, sees all moments simultaneously, knows all secrets, and calls conscious beings into relationship.

Why it matters: This metaphor emphasizes the personal nature of ultimate truth. The goal of existence is not to merge into an undifferentiated cosmic consciousness but to enter into direct relationship with the divine. You are known as a unique individual, loved as yourself, called by name.

How to work with it: Practice relating to the divine as a person rather than a concept. Speak to the Architect in prayer. Listen for the Architect's voice in silence. Look for the Architect's presence in your daily life. Notice how this personal relationship differs from abstract philosophical understanding.

THE WITNESS

The witness is human consciousness in its role of observing and thereby actualizing reality. You are the witness—the awareness that turns on the lights, names the colors, brings potential into actuality. The witness is not separate from what is witnessed but participates in its reality.

Why it matters: This metaphor emphasizes your essential role in the cosmos. You are not an accident or an afterthought. Your consciousness matters. Your witnessing is a sacred act that participates in the ongoing creation of reality.

How to work with it: Practice pure witnessing—observing your experience without immediately judging, categorizing, or reacting. Notice the difference between the content of consciousness (thoughts, sensations, emotions) and the awareness that witnesses them. Can you rest in the witnessing itself?

THE WEB OF CONSCIOUSNESS/INDRA'S NET

The web of consciousness or Indra's Net represents the fundamental interconnection of all beings. Like a web where each strand touches all others, or like a net of jewels where each reflects all the others, consciousness is not isolated in separate individuals but is a unified field expressing itself through particular forms.

Why it matters: This metaphor challenges the illusion of separation and reveals our deep connection to all beings. What happens to one affects all. Your flourishing and the flourishing of the whole are not separate. This understanding transforms ethics, compassion, and our sense of responsibility.

How to work with it: Practice recognizing your connection to others. When you encounter someone, try seeing them not as a separate, isolated individual but as another expression of the same consciousness that expresses itself through you. Notice how this shifts your perception and your behavior.

THE ETERNAL REWARD

The eternal reward is not a prize earned through good behavior but the relationship with the Architect that transcends physical existence. It is direct knowledge of the divine, perfect union, the dissolution of all mystery and separation. It is what remains when the classroom dissolves and the grand illusion of matter ends.

Why it matters: This metaphor provides ultimate purpose and hope. The struggles of this life are not meaningless. The lessons learned in the classroom prepare you for something beyond imagination. Death is not the end but graduation into fuller reality.

How to work with it: Practice living with eternity in view. When making decisions, ask: How does this choice align with my ultimate destination? What am I developing in myself that will transcend this temporary existence? This doesn't mean neglecting present responsibilities, but holding them in the context of eternal purpose.

THE RETURN/COMING HOME

The return or homecoming represents the spiritual journey's paradoxical nature: the destination is the starting point. You are seeking what you have never lost, traveling toward where you have always been. Coming home to the Architect is recognizing the union that has never been broken.

Why it matters: This metaphor prevents spiritual striving from becoming another form of grasping. You are not trying to become something you are not or achieve something you lack. You are remembering what is already true, awakening to what has always been the case.

How to work with it: Practice remembering rather than achieving. Instead of asking "How can I reach enlightenment?" ask "What am I forgetting?" Instead of striving to become spiritual, notice the ways you are already held by the divine. The practice is not acquisition but recognition.

May these metaphors serve as doorways rather than destinations, as fingers pointing at the moon rather than the moon itself. May they help you recognize the truth of your being and come home to the Architect who has been calling you all along.

FOOTNOTES

CHAPTER 1:
THE VOID AND THE WITNESS

THE HARD PROBLEM OF CONSCIOUSNESS

1. Chalmers, David J. *The Conscious Mind: In Search of a Fundamental Theory*. Oxford University Press, 1996. Chalmers distinguishes between the "easy problems" of consciousness (explaining cognitive functions and behaviors) and the "hard problem" (explaining why there is subjective experience at all—why information processing feels like something from the inside).

2. The double-slit experiment demonstrates that observation affects quantum behavior. When electrons pass through two slits without being observed, they create an interference pattern characteristic of waves. When observed, they behave as particles. This suggests consciousness plays a role in actualizing quantum reality. See Feynman, Richard P. *The Feynman Lectures on Physics, Vol. III*. Addison-Wesley, 1965.

PARTICIPATORY UNIVERSE

1. Wheeler, John Archibald. "The 'Past' and the 'Delayed-Choice' Double-Slit Experiment." In *Mathematical Foundations of Quantum Theory*, edited by A.R. Marlow, 9-48. Academic Press, 1978. Wheeler's delayed-choice quantum eraser experiment suggests that observation in the present can affect what "happened" in the past, supporting the idea that consciousness participates in creating reality rather than passively observing it.

2. Wheeler, John Archibald. "Law Without Law." In *Quantum*

Theory and Measurement, edited by John Archibald Wheeler and Wojciech Hubert Zurek, 182-213. Princeton University Press, 1983. Wheeler's participatory anthropic principle proposes that observers are necessary to bring the universe into being.

PHILOSOPHICAL FOUNDATIONS

1. Kant, Immanuel. *Critique of Pure Reason.* Translated by Paul Guyer and Allen W. Wood. Cambridge University Press, 1998 [1781/1787]. Kant's transcendental idealism argues that we cannot know things-in-themselves (noumena), only things as they appear to us through the structures of consciousness (phenomena). The blue ball metaphor draws on this distinction.

2. Gadamer, Hans-Georg. *Truth and Method.* Translated by Joel Weinsheimer and Donald G. Marshall. Continuum, 2004 [1960]. Gadamer's hermeneutical philosophy emphasizes that understanding is not passive reception but active interpretation shaped by the interpreter's horizon of meaning.

CHAPTER 2:
THE SCRIPT OF THE BLOCK UNIVERSE

RELATIVITY AND SPACETIME

1. Einstein, Albert. "On the Electrodynamics of Moving Bodies." *Annalen der Physik* 17 (1905): 891-921. Einstein's special theory of relativity demonstrates that simultaneity is relative to the observer's frame of reference, undermining the absolute distinction between past, present, and future.

2. Minkowski, Hermann. "Space and Time." In *The Principle of Relativity*, translated by W. Perrett and G.B. Jeffery, 75-91. Dover, 1952 [1907]. Minkowski's mathematical formulation presents spacetime as a four-dimensional manifold in which all events exist eternally: "Henceforth space by itself, and time by itself, are doomed to fade away into mere shadows, and only a kind of union of the two will preserve an independent reality."

3. Penrose, Roger. *The Road to Reality: A Complete Guide to the Laws of the Universe*. Alfred A. Knopf, 2005. Penrose discusses the Block Universe interpretation of relativity, in which past, present, and future are equally real and the flow of time is an illusion of consciousness.

PHILOSOPHY OF TIME

1. McTaggart, J.M.E. "The Unreality of Time." *Mind* 17, no. 68 (1908): 457-474. McTaggart's famous argument distinguishes between the A-series (past, present, future) and B-series (earlier than, simultaneous with, later than) and argues that time is ultimately unreal.

2. Lewis, David. *On the Plurality of Worlds*. Blackwell, 1986. Lewis's modal realism treats possible worlds as equally real, analogous to how the Block Universe treats all temporal moments as equally real.

PERSONAL IDENTITY AND TIME

1. Parfit, Derek. *Reasons and Persons*. Oxford University Press, 1984. Parfit explores personal identity in a four-dimensional universe, arguing that what matters is not strict identity over time but psychological continuity and connectedness.

DETERMINISM AND FREEDOM

1. Frankfurt, Harry G. "Alternate Possibilities and Moral Responsibility." *Journal of Philosophy* 66, no. 23 (1969): 829-839. Frankfurt's compatibilist argument that moral responsibility does not require the ability to do otherwise informs the discussion of freedom within determinism.

2. Dennett, Daniel C. *Elbow Room: The Varieties of Free Will Worth Wanting*. MIT Press, 1984. Dennett defends compatibilism, arguing that the kind of freedom worth having is compatible with determinism.

CHAPTER 3:
THE HIDDEN VARIABLE

BIBLICAL FOUNDATIONS

1. *The Holy Bible, New International Version.* Zondervan, 2011. Key passages:
   a. John 1:1: "In the beginning was the Word, and the Word was with God, and the Word was God."
   b. Hebrews 4:13: "Nothing in all creation is hidden from God's sight. Everything is uncovered and laid bare before the eyes of him to whom we must give account."
   c. Psalm 139:1-4: "You have searched me, Lord, and you know me. You know when I sit and when I rise; you perceive my thoughts from afar..."

DIVINE OMNISCIENCE

1. Augustine of Hippo. *Confessions.* Translated by Henry Chadwick. Oxford University Press, 2008 [397-400 CE]. Augustine explores the paradox of divine foreknowledge and human freedom, arguing that God's knowledge exists outside time and therefore does not causally determine human choices.
2. Aquinas, Thomas. *Summa Theologica*, I, Q.14. Translated by Fathers of the English Dominican Province. Benziger Bros., 1947 [1265-1274]. Aquinas argues that God knows all things—past, present, and future—in a single eternal act of knowing, seeing all temporal moments simultaneously from the perspective of eternity.
3. Boethius. *The Consolation of Philosophy.* Translated by V.E. Watts. Penguin Classics, 1999 [524 CE]. Book V addresses how God's eternal knowledge is compatible with human freedom: God sees all moments of time simultaneously in an eternal present, so divine foreknowledge does not impose necessity on future events.

THEOLOGICAL DEBATES

1. Molina, Luis de. *On Divine Foreknowledge (Part IV of the Concordia)*. Translated by Alfred J. Freddoso. Cornell University Press, 1988 [1588]. Molina's doctrine of "middle knowledge" attempts to reconcile divine omniscience with libertarian free will.

2. Bañez, Domingo. *Scholastica Commentaria in Primam Partem Summae Theologicae S. Thomae Aquinatis*. Madrid, 1584-1588. Bañez defends Thomistic predetermination against Molina, arguing that God's knowledge includes efficacious decrees that determine all events.

CHAPTER 4:
GRADUATION AND THE GREATER DESTINATION

PHYSICS AND COSMOLOGY

1. Clausius, Rudolf. "On the Moving Force of Heat." *Annalen der Physik* 79 (1850): 368-397, 500-524. Clausius formulated the second law of thermodynamics, establishing that entropy (disorder) increases in closed systems over time.

2. Adams, Fred C., and Gregory Laughlin. "A Dying Universe: The Long-Term Fate and Evolution of Astrophysical Objects." *Reviews of Modern Physics* 69, no. 2 (1997): 337-372. Discusses the heat death of the universe as the ultimate state of maximum entropy.

3. Penrose, Roger. *Cycles of Time: An Extraordinary New View of the Universe.* Bodley Head, 2010. Penrose's Conformal Cyclic Cosmology (CCC) hypothesis proposes that the universe undergoes infinite cycles, with each "aeon" beginning with a Big Bang and ending in infinite expansion.

THEOLOGICAL PERSPECTIVES

1. Aquinas, Thomas. *Summa Theologica*, I, Q.46, Art.2. Aquinas argues that while reason cannot prove the world had a beginning, revelation teaches that creation is temporal and will have an end, after which the blessed will enjoy eternal beatitude.

2. Eckhart, Meister. *The Complete Mystical Works of Meister Eckhart.* Translated by Maurice O'C. Walshe. Crossroad, 2009. Eckhart describes the transcendent "ground of being" beyond all created things, the eternal reality that precedes and exceeds the temporal universe.

ESCHATOLOGY

1. Moltmann, Jürgen. *Theology of Hope: On the Ground and the Implications of a Christian Eschatology.* Translated by James W.

Leitch. Harper & Row, 1967. Moltmann presents Christian hope as oriented toward God's future kingdom that transcends and transforms temporal history.

CHAPTER 5:
THE ETERNAL REWARD

BIBLICAL AND THEOLOGICAL FOUNDATIONS

1. John 17:3: "Now this is eternal life: that they know you, the only true God, and Jesus Christ, whom you have sent." This verse establishes eternal life as relational knowledge rather than mere duration.

2. Buber, Martin. *I and Thou*. Translated by Walter Kaufmann. Scribner, 1970 [1923]. Buber distinguishes between I-It relationships (objectifying, instrumental) and I-Thou relationships (dialogical, mutual, personal). God is the eternal Thou who can never be reduced to an It.

3. Marcel, Gabriel. *The Mystery of Being*. Translated by G.S. Fraser and René Hague. Gateway Editions, 1950. Marcel explores the distinction between problems (which can be solved objectively) and mysteries (which involve the questioner and cannot be objectified), arguing that ultimate reality is mystery requiring participation rather than detached analysis.

DIVINE LOVE

1. Nygren, Anders. *Agape and Eros*. Translated by Philip S. Watson. Westminster Press, 1953. Nygren analyzes the distinctive character of Christian agape (self-giving, unconditional love) as contrasted with eros (desire, acquisitive love).

2. Augustine of Hippo. *On the Trinity*. Translated by Edmund Hill. New City Press, 1991 [400-416 CE]. Augustine explores the Incarnation as the supreme manifestation of divine love, God becoming human to restore relationship with humanity.

UNION WITH GOD

1. Gregory of Nyssa. *The Life of Moses.* Translated by Abraham J. Malherbe and Everett Ferguson. Paulist Press, 1978 [c. 390 CE]. Gregory describes theosis (deification or union with God) as the goal of Christian life, an infinite progress into divine mystery.

CHAPTER 6:
THE ARCHITECTURE OF SUFFERING

THE PROBLEM OF EVIL

1. Leibniz, Gottfried Wilhelm. *Theodicy: Essays on the Goodness of God, the Freedom of Man, and the Origin of Evil.* Translated by E.M. Huggard. Open Court, 1985 [1710]. Leibniz argues that this is "the best of all possible worlds" because God, being perfectly good and omnipotent, would create the best possible world, and any world containing free beings must allow for the possibility of evil.

2. Hick, John. *Evil and the God of Love.* Harper & Row, 1966. Hick develops an "Irenaean" theodicy (as opposed to Augustinian), arguing that the world is a "vale of soul-making" where suffering serves the purpose of spiritual development.

3. Plantinga, Alvin. *God, Freedom, and Evil.* Eerdmans, 1974. Plantinga's free will defense argues that it is logically possible that God could not create a world with free creatures who never choose evil.

PROCESS THEOLOGY

1. Whitehead, Alfred North. *Process and Reality: An Essay in Cosmology.* Corrected edition, edited by David Ray Griffin and Donald W. Sherburne. Free Press, 1978 [1929]. Whitehead's process philosophy presents God as persuasive rather than coercive, working within the constraints of creaturely freedom and natural law.

SUFFERING AND SPIRITUAL GROWTH

1. John of the Cross. *Dark Night of the Soul.* Translated by E. Allison Peers. Image Books, 1959 [1578-1579]. John describes the "dark night" as a necessary stage of spiritual purification in which God strips away attachments and false consolations to prepare the soul for union.

2. Frankl, Viktor E. *Man's Search for Meaning*. Beacon Press, 2006 [1946]. Frankl, a Holocaust survivor and psychiatrist, argues that meaning can be found even in the most extreme suffering, and that the search for meaning is the primary human motivation.

3. Lewis, C.S. *The Problem of Pain*. HarperOne, 2001 [1940]. Lewis explores how suffering can be compatible with divine love, arguing that pain is God's "megaphone to rouse a deaf world" and a tool for spiritual refinement.

SOLIDARITY AND COMPASSION

1. Sölle, Dorothee. *Suffering*. Translated by Everett R. Kalin. Fortress Press, 1975. Sölle critiques theodicies that justify suffering and instead emphasizes solidarity with those who suffer and resistance to unjust suffering.

CHAPTER 7:
THE ILLUSION OF SEPARATION

BUDDHIST PHILOSOPHY

1. *Anatta* (no-self) is a central doctrine in Buddhism, teaching that there is no permanent, unchanging self. See Rahula, Walpola. *What the Buddha Taught*. Grove Press, 1974.

2. *Avatamsaka Sutra* (Flower Garland Sutra). Translated by Thomas Cleary. Shambhala, 1993. This Mahayana Buddhist text presents the metaphor of Indra's Net, in which each jewel reflects all other jewels, symbolizing the interpenetration and mutual containment of all phenomena.

3. Nhat Hanh, Thich. *The Heart of Understanding: Commentaries on the Prajnaparamita Heart Sutra*. Parallax Press, 1988. Thich Nhat Hanh introduces the concept of "interbeing"—the recognition that nothing exists independently but only in relationship to everything else.

CONTEMPORARY SCIENCE

1. Sheldrake, Rupert. *The Presence of the Past: Morphic Resonance and the Habits of Nature*. Park Street Press, 1988. Sheldrake proposes that natural systems inherit a collective memory through morphic resonance, suggesting a form of non-local connection across space and time.

2. Rizzolatti, Giacomo, and Laila Craighero. "The Mirror-Neuron System." *Annual Review of Neuroscience* 27 (2004): 169-192. Mirror neurons fire both when an individual performs an action and when they observe another performing the same action, suggesting a neurological basis for empathy and interconnection.

3. Varela, Francisco J., Evan Thompson, and Eleanor Rosch. *The Embodied Mind: Cognitive Science and Human Experience*. MIT

Press, 1991. Explores embodied cognition and the ways consciousness is fundamentally relational and embedded in the world.

SYSTEMS THEORY

1. Bertalanffy, Ludwig von. *General System Theory: Foundations, Development, Applications*. George Braziller, 1968. Bertalanffy's systems theory emphasizes holistic interconnection and the principle that the whole is greater than the sum of its parts.

QUANTUM PHYSICS

1. Bell, John S. „On the Einstein Podolsky Rosen Paradox." *Physics* 1, no. 3 (1964): 195-200. Bell's theorem demonstrates that quantum entanglement creates correlations between particles that cannot be explained by local hidden variables, suggesting non-local connections.

ADVAITA VEDANTA

1. Shankara. *Crest-Jewel of Discrimination (Viveka-Chudamani)*. Translated by Swami Prabhavananda and Christopher Isherwood. Vedanta Press, 1978 [8th century CE]. Shankara's non-dual Vedanta teaches that Atman (individual self) and Brahman (universal consciousness) are ultimately identical.

CHAPTER 8:
THE PRACTICE OF PRESENCE

CHRISTIAN CONTEMPLATIVE TRADITION

1. *The Cloud of Unknowing*. Translated by Carmen Acevedo Butcher. Shambhala, 2009 [14th century]. This anonymous Christian mystical text teaches contemplative prayer as resting in God's presence beyond thoughts and images.

2. Merton, Thomas. *The Inner Experience: Notes on Contemplation*. Edited by William H. Shannon. HarperOne, 2003. Merton explores contemplative awareness as direct, non-conceptual knowledge of God and one's true self.

3. Keating, Thomas. *Open Mind, Open Heart: The Contemplative Dimension of the Gospel*. Continuum, 1986. Keating presents Centering Prayer as a method of contemplative practice rooted in Christian tradition.

EASTERN ORTHODOX TRADITION

1. Evagrius Ponticus. *The Praktikos & Chapters on Prayer*. Translated by John Eudes Bamberger. Cistercian Publications, 1981 [4th century]. Evagrius teaches hesychia (stillness) as the foundation of prayer and spiritual transformation.

2. *The Way of a Pilgrim*. Translated by R.M. French. HarperOne, 1991 [19th century]. This Russian Orthodox classic describes the practice of the Jesus Prayer ("Lord Jesus Christ, have mercy on me") as a path to unceasing prayer and presence.

MINDFULNESS AND MEDITATION

1. Nhat Hanh, Thich. *The Miracle of Mindfulness: An Introduction to the Practice of Meditation*. Beacon Press, 1975. Thich Nhat Hanh presents mindfulness as bringing full attention to the present moment in everyday activities.

2. Kabat-Zinn, Jon. *Wherever You Go, There You Are: Mindfulness Meditation in Everyday Life*. Hyperion, 1994. Kabat-Zinn, founder of Mindfulness-Based Stress Reduction (MBSR), presents secular mindfulness practice grounded in Buddhist meditation.

NEUROSCIENCE OF MEDITATION

1. Davidson, Richard J., and Antoine Lutz. "Buddha's Brain: Neuroplasticity and Meditation." *IEEE Signal Processing Magazine* 25, no. 1 (2008): 176-174. Reviews neuroscientific research demonstrating that meditation practice produces measurable changes in brain structure and function.

2. Tang, Yi-Yuan, Britta K. Hölzel, and Michael I. Posner. "The Neuroscience of Mindfulness Meditation." *Nature Reviews Neuroscience* 16 (2015): 213-225. Comprehensive review of neuroplasticity and attention training through meditation.

CHAPTER 9:
THE PROBLEM OF PARADOX

COINCIDENCE OF OPPOSITES

1. Nicholas of Cusa. *On Learned Ignorance (De Docta Ignorantia)*. Translated by Jasper Hopkins. Arthur J. Banning Press, 1985 [1440]. Nicholas introduces the concept of *coincidentia oppositorum* (coincidence of opposites), arguing that in God all contradictions are reconciled and that human knowledge must embrace paradox when approaching the infinite.

APOPHATIC THEOLOGY

1. Pseudo-Dionysius the Areopagite. *The Complete Works*. Translated by Colm Luibheid. Paulist Press, 1987 [c. 500 CE]. Pseudo-Dionysius develops negative (apophatic) theology, arguing that God transcends all affirmations and negations, and can only be approached through unknowing.

ZEN BUDDHISM

1. Aitken, Robert. *Taking the Path of Zen*. North Point Press, 1982. Aitken explains how Zen koans use paradox to break through conceptual thinking and catalyze direct insight.
2. Suzuki, D.T. *An Introduction to Zen Buddhism*. Grove Press, 1964. Suzuki explores how Zen uses paradox and contradiction to point beyond dualistic thinking.

QUANTUM COMPLEMENTARITY

1. Bohr, Niels. "The Quantum Postulate and the Recent Development of Atomic Theory." *Nature* 121 (1928): 580-590. Bohr introduces the principle of complementarity: wave and particle descriptions of light are mutually exclusive yet both necessary for complete understanding.

2. Heisenberg, Werner. *Physics and Philosophy: The Revolution in Modern Science.* Harper & Row, 1958. Heisenberg explores the philosophical implications of quantum mechanics, including the role of paradox and complementarity.

DIALECTICAL PHILOSOPHY

1. Hegel, G.W.F. *Phenomenology of Spirit.* Translated by A.V. Miller. Oxford University Press, 1977 [1807]. Hegel's dialectical method moves through thesis, antithesis, and synthesis, showing how contradictions are resolved at higher levels of understanding.

INTEGRAL THEORY

1. Wilber, Ken. *A Theory of Everything: An Integral Vision for Business, Politics, Science, and Spirituality.* Shambhala, 2000. Wilber's integral approach attempts to honor multiple perspectives and transcend either/or thinking through both/and integration.

IMPLICATE AND EXPLICATE ORDER

1. Bohm, David. *Wholeness and the Implicate Order.* Routledge, 1980. Bohm proposes that reality consists of an implicate (enfolded) order underlying the explicate (unfolded) order we perceive, reconciling quantum wholeness with classical separateness.

CHAPTER 10:
THE RETURN

MYSTICAL STAGES

1. Teresa of Avila. *The Interior Castle*. Translated by Mirabai Starr. Riverhead Books, 2003 [1577]. Teresa describes seven "mansions" or stages of spiritual development, culminating in mystical marriage (union with God).

2. John of the Cross. *The Ascent of Mount Carmel* and *The Dark Night of the Soul*. Translated by E. Allison Peers. Image Books, 1959 [1578-1579]. John maps the spiritual journey through purgation, illumination, and union, emphasizing the necessity of the dark night for transformation.

3. Underhill, Evelyn. *Mysticism: A Study in the Nature and Development of Spiritual Consciousness*. Dover, 2002 [1911]. Underhill identifies five stages of mystical development: awakening, purgation, illumination, dark night, and union.

THE RETURN

1. Eliot, T.S. *Four Quartets*. Harcourt, 1943. Eliot's "Little Gidding" contains the famous lines: "We shall not cease from exploration/ And the end of all our exploring/Will be to arrive where we started/And know the place for the first time."

2. Eckhart, Meister. *Sermons and Treatises, Volume I*. Translated by M. O'C. Walshe. Element Books, 1987. Eckhart teaches *Gelassenheit* (releasement or letting-go) and describes the soul's return to the divine ground from which it never truly departed.

NEOPLATONISM

1. Plotinus. *The Enneads*. Translated by Stephen MacKenna. Penguin Classics, 1991 [3rd century CE]. Plotinus describes the soul's emanation from the One and its return through contemplation and purification.

DEVELOPMENTAL PSYCHOLOGY

1. Kegan, Robert. *The Evolving Self: Problem and Process in Human Development.* Harvard University Press, 1982. Kegan presents a stage theory of ego development showing how consciousness evolves through increasingly complex meaning-making structures.

2. Beck, Don Edward, and Christopher C. Cowan. *Spiral Dynamics: Mastering Values, Leadership, and Change.* Blackwell, 1996. Presents a spiral model of human development through value systems (memes), emphasizing that development is not linear but involves returning to earlier themes at higher levels of integration.

Note to Readers: These footnotes are provided for those who wish to explore the philosophical, theological, and scientific foundations of the ideas presented in this book. They are not exhaustive but represent key sources and entry points for further study. The absence of a citation does not indicate lack of influence—many ideas emerge from years of reading, conversation, and contemplation that cannot be traced to single sources. Where possible, I have acknowledged debts and pointed toward resources for deeper investigation.

SUPPLEMENTARY NOTES AND SOURCES

ON LANGUAGE AND THEOLOGY

1. Note on Gendered Pronouns: This text uses masculine pronouns for the Architect following traditional Christian theological language. However, the author acknowledges that ultimate reality transcends all human categories including gender. As Gregory of Nyssa wrote, "The divine nature, whatever it may be in itself, surpasses every mental concept" (*On the Making of Man*, 11). Feminine and non-gendered language for God has rich precedent in mystical traditions (Julian of Norwich's "God our Mother," the Shekinah in Jewish mysticism).

2. Panentheism vs. Classical Theism: This book draws significantly on panentheistic theology—the view that God is both transcendent (beyond creation) and immanent (present within creation), that the universe exists within God while God exceeds the universe. This differs from classical theism's emphasis on divine transcendence and from pantheism's identification of God with the universe. See Clayton, Philip, and Arthur Peacocke, eds. *In Whom We Live and Move and Have Our Being: Panentheistic Reflections on God's Presence in a Scientific World*. Eerdmans, 2004.

3. Process Theology: The book's emphasis on divine persuasion rather than coercion, on becoming rather than static being, and on God's relationship to time draws on process theology. See Cobb, John B., Jr., and David Ray Griffin. *Process Theology: An Introductory Exposition*. Westminster Press, 1976.

ON METAPHORS AND THEIR SOURCES

1. **The Blue Ball Thought Experiment:** This is original to this work but informed by quantum observation experiments (particularly the double-slit experiment and Wheeler's delayed-choice experiment) and phenomenological philosophy (Husserl, Heidegger, Merleau-Ponty on the relationship between consciousness and world).

2. **The Block Universe:** Based on the physics of special and general relativity (Einstein, Minkowski) and philosophical interpretations of spacetime (McTaggart, Penrose, Putnam). See Putnam, Hilary. "Time and Physical Geometry." *Journal of Philosophy* 64, no. 8 (1967): 240-247.

3. **The Classroom Universe:** This pedagogical metaphor has roots in Irenaeus of Lyon's theology of spiritual development, John Hick's "soul-making theodicy," and process theology's emphasis on creative transformation. See Irenaeus. *Against Heresies.* Translated by Alexander Roberts and William Rambaut. Aeterna Press, 2016 [c. 180 CE].

4. **The Witness:** Influenced by phenomenology (Husserl's transcendental ego, Heidegger's Dasein), consciousness studies (Chalmers, Nagel), and contemplative traditions (the "witness consciousness" in Vedanta, *shikantaza* or "just sitting" in Zen, *prosoche* or attention in Stoicism).

5. **Indra's Net:** From the *Avatamsaka Sutra* in Huayan Buddhism, used to illustrate the interpenetration of all phenomena. See Cook, Francis H. *Hua-Yen Buddhism: The Jewel Net of Indra.* Pennsylvania State University Press, 1977.

6. **The Void/Darkness:** Influenced by apophatic theology (Pseudo-Dionysius, *The Cloud of Unknowing*), the mystical darkness in John of the Cross, and the Buddhist concept of śūn*yat*ā (emptiness). The void is not nihilistic absence but pregnant potentiality.

Primary Texts for Further Study

BIBLICAL TEXTS

1. *Gospel of John* (especially Prologue 1:1-18 and High Priestly Prayer in Chapter 17)
2. *Romans 8* (on the Spirit, suffering, and hope)
3. *1 Corinthians 13* (on love as the greatest virtue)
4. *Ephesians 1* (on God's eternal plan and cosmic reconciliation)

MYSTICAL AND CONTEMPLATIVE TEXTS

5. *The Cloud of Unknowing* (14th century, anonymous)
6. Eckhart, Meister. *Selected Writings*
7. Teresa of Avila. *The Interior Castle*
8. John of the Cross. *Dark Night of the Soul* and *The Ascent of Mount Carmel*
9. Julian of Norwich. *Revelations of Divine Love*

PHILOSOPHICAL TEXTS

10. Plato. *Timaeus* (on the divine craftsman and creation)
11. Plotinus. *The Enneads* (on emanation and return to the One)
12. Whitehead, Alfred North. *Process and Reality*
13. Heidegger, Martin. *Being and Time*
14. Levinas, Emmanuel. *Totality and Infinity* (on the face of the Other and ethical relationship)

SCIENTIFIC TEXTS

15. Einstein, Albert. *Relativity: The Special and General Theory*
16. Heisenberg, Werner. *Physics and Philosophy*

17. Bohr, Niels. *Atomic Physics and Human Knowledge*

18. Penrose, Roger. *The Emperor's New Mind* (on consciousness and physics)

CONTEMPORARY THEOLOGY AND PHILOSOPHY

19. Teilhard de Chardin, Pierre. *The Phenomenon of Man*. Harper & Row, 1959. Teilhard's vision of cosmic evolution toward the Omega Point (Christ as the goal of evolution).

20. Rahner, Karl. *Foundations of Christian Faith*. Crossroad, 1978. Rahner's transcendental theology and concept of the "supernatural existential."

21. Moltmann, Jürgen. *The Trinity and the Kingdom*. Fortress Press, 1993. Social trinitarianism and perichoresis (mutual indwelling).

22. Pannenberg, Wolfhart. *Systematic Theology, Volume 1*. Eerdmans, 1991. On God's futurity and the relationship between time and eternity.

ON THE RELATIONSHIP BETWEEN SCIENCE AND THEOLOGY

23. **Methodological Naturalism:** Science operates through methodological naturalism (explaining phenomena through natural causes) without requiring metaphysical naturalism (the claim that only natural things exist). This book assumes science and theology address different but complementary questions. See Plantinga, Alvin. *Where the Conflict Really Lies: Science, Religion, and Naturalism*. Oxford University Press, 2011.

24. **Fine-Tuning:** The precise values of physical constants necessary for life suggest intentionality without constituting scientific proof of God. See Barrow, John D., and Frank J. Tipler. *The Anthropic Cosmological Principle*. Oxford University Press, 1986. Also Collins, Robin. "The Teleological Argument: An Exploration of the Fine-Tuning of the Universe." In *The Blackwell Companion to*

Natural Theology, edited by William Lane Craig and J.P. Moreland, 202-281. Wiley-Blackwell, 2009.

25. **Complementarity of Ways of Knowing:** Science provides empirical, quantitative knowledge of physical mechanisms. Theology and philosophy provide interpretive frameworks for meaning, purpose, and value. Both are necessary for comprehensive understanding. See Polkinghorne, John. *Belief in God in an Age of Science*. Yale University Press, 1998.

PERSONAL TESTIMONY: THE AUTHOR'S WITNESS

My Conscience cannot leave you without confessing my own testimony. You have the power and freedom to search for any destination you desire. This is my personal testimony written on My Heart, My Soul and My Mind. In my lifetime I have had many revelations come during my spiritual growth with God. Sixty-four years in the classroom at this time. I hope for many more revelations.

I have said often during this book that what you are searching for was always with you in the beginning. In fact, the very first words that are read at the start of this journey is:

> "In the beginning was the Word, and the Word was with God, and the Word was God,"
>
> John 1:1

Pause here and really think about what this means.

Before the Big Bang, the creation of the Universe, our classroom, something existed and has always existed in the Beyond.

"The Word"

What is this Word?

The Answer?

After all the words that filled the pages of this book, I can honestly testify this is The Answer. The definite Answer to the Beyond. After all the scaffolding is gone, and nothing of the material universe is left. All there is left is The Beyond.

God loves you so much he provided the ultimate Grace. I challenge you and pray that you search for the following on your own.

THIS IS THE TRUTH: "The Word became flesh and dwelt among us" (John 1:14) is the foundational Christian theological statement describing the Incarnation—God becoming human in the person of Jesus Christ.